Whole Hearted

Whole Hearted

Applied Spirituality for Everyday Life

THE COLLECTED WISDOM OF
SWAMI VEDA BHARATI

Contents

Introduction: What Good is a Spiritual Life?

W hat good is a spiritual life? This might sound like an odd question coming from someone who has taken the vows of a swami, who lives at an ashram, who has lectured and written on the power of meditation for decades, and who has devoted his life to the spiritual path.

But, really—what good is it? Is it to get you into Heaven? Is it to impress others with how pious you are? Is it to make you feel "above it all"?" Is it to help you be a magnetic personality and get ahead in your chosen work? If so, it is useless. For if our personal and professional lives remain separate from our spiritual life, there is no spiritual life. If our spirituality does not benefit many and does not comfort many, what is the difference between a spiritual life and a selfish material life? No difference at all.

In March 2013, I took an additional vow. It is a vow of silence meant to last five years, or perhaps even longer. But because so many people requested it—and because, of course, I did not mind having a "last word"—I wrote a small book on the subject of applied spirituality. It was humbly offered as a set of guidelines for those who work within the large international organization that I head. The book became quite popular and many have asked me to offer it again, but with a few embellishments for the general reader. By "general reader," I mean anyone who has an interest in pursuing a spiritual connection, especially through the art and science of meditation, but who, like most practitioners, struggles with practical "real-life" issues that sometimes leave them wondering: *Why can't I carry the serenity and joy I experience during practice into my relationships, my workplace, and my community?*

I'll tell you why: Because there are other people involved in each of these settings! It is easy to feel saintly all alone on your meditation cushion, but try taking a phone call the minute your sitting ends—from your boss, or your ex-boyfriend or girlfriend, or your mother-in-law, or your tax accountant. Suddenly you are not such a saint anymore. You are emotional. You are reactive. Dare I say, you are a mess.

This book is meant as a tool to make your "real life" an extension of your spiritual life, so that life will be less messy—and more productive and enjoyable—overall. It starts by discussing what meditation is really for, then suggests some ways of dealing with the other people in your life based on what you learn from your practice. It then addresses several of the emotional resistances you will no doubt have to following what is, essentially, very simple advice.

Just because something is simple does not mean it is easy—far from it. But at no point in this book will I ask you to deal with complicated philosophy. My philosophy really could not be more straightforward. I see my being—and the essence of your being, and of all our beings—as pure spirit that is unborn and therefore immortal, continuing from infinity to infinity.

Spirit is the One with whom I truly identify. That is what I am. That is what you are.

Too often we set that realization aside when we are not "actively" meditating. We ask, *What does it have to do with me right here, right now? It's too ethereal. I have to pay the bills, return my calls, and be practical.* But that attitude is missing the point.

Let's consider the question again. What does this realization have to do with right now? Only everything. It is when we forget this basic truth that all of our problems begin.

One

WHAT IS MEDITATION FOR?

If you are reading this book, you probably have some interest in meditation. You may have a regular meditation practice or, more commonly, an irregular one. But why did you become interested in meditation in the first place?

Some may say it is because they wanted to calm down; others may say it is because they wanted to improve their concentration; others may say they wanted to enhance their imagination and creativity; and still others will say they wanted to feel a connection to something larger than themselves. These are all good reasons. (Truthfully, I have yet to come across a bad reason!)

In a nutshell, meditation is the art and science of self-governance. My tradition, the Himalayan tradition, is a very practical one. It does not merely teach techniques for meditation, but teaches the methods whereby one's meditation practice may be applied to cultivate, enhance, and beautify one's personality, leading to very practical benefits in personal, interpersonal, and even corporate life.

Do you want to learn self-control? It is not possible to exercise true self-control and to conquer one's senses without the practice of meditation. Do you want to gain wisdom? Through meditation one gains access to one's own inner gates of wisdom. Do you want to achieve certain meaningful goals? To quote a fourth-century sage known as Chanakya, whose words are as true today as they ever were, "One who has conquered the self finds all his purposes and goals being accomplished."

What does all of this conquest of the senses and attainment of intuitive wisdom have to do with success in the business world, where we always have to push, compete, assert ourselves, and even fight? The wisdom of the sages says that it is not necessary to take such an aggressive stance in order to succeed.

Let me tell you the story of a Mughal emperor, Akbar, and his wise minister named Virbal. All the courtiers were jealous of Virbal because he was obviously the emperor's favorite. They asked the emperor why: "What does Virbal have that we do not have?" The emperor promised to answer the question on some other day.

One morning, as his courtiers arrived, the emperor posed a question to them. He drew a line on the board and asked them to "make the line shorter." Easy! Everyone attempted to rush to the blackboard, and one of them managed to erase a part of the line.

The emperor said, "No, no. Shorten the line, but do not touch it!"

Well, that was indeed a puzzle. Nobody could solve the problem. The emperor finally beckoned to Virbal to "come make my line shorter without touching it." Virbal quietly got up, took a piece of chalk, and drew a parallel line:

_____ the emperor's line

_____ Virbal's line

"Your line is shorter, Your Majesty," Virbal declared.

In the act there was no need to diminish the work of another, no need to compete. Virbal went deep within himself (this is meditation!) for the answer and devoted himself to the task at hand. Whoever is fully restrained, in possession of his senses and emotions, acts constructively and in all humility. Whoever learns from the wise will doubtless achieve "success without competing."

We can say much more about this topic, but that would make a book of its own. Here we come to the question of the right system of meditation for accomplishing a personal self that can navigate a path such as Virbal's. There are many systems of meditation. Which should we choose? As a keeper of my tradition, I propose and teach the Himalayan system.

The Jigsaw Puzzle of Himalayan Meditation

There are many meditation traditions around the world. In fact, it is a testament to the merit of meditation that so many civilizations have considered it such an essential aspect of life. Himalayan meditation is a comprehensive system that excludes none of the authentic major traditions of meditation. For example, the Vipassana system teaches us to concentrate on breath flow and body awareness, to start with, but does not use a mantra for focus. Transcendental meditation uses a mantra, but not breath awareness. Zen has a certain method of dealing with random thoughts. In the Himalayan system, we use all of these methods, and more, to form a complete picture. Someone schooled in this approach has been taught the right place for each technique and where it fits into the larger frame. (For more on this, please see my short writings, *Beginning Meditation* and *The Himalayan Tradition of Yoga Meditation*.)

The teachers of the Himalayan tradition have gathered tremendous experience and expertise that has been handed down for over forty centuries. And because well-trained teachers are familiar with many other systems of meditation, and are able to work with people of all religions and backgrounds, they may lead students on specialized paths according to their emotional needs. For example, a person needing emotional strength will be advised to concentrate on the cardiac center, while an intellectually inclined person may focus on the center between the eyebrows.

Himalayan meditation works on all the different components of one's personality. It encompasses the spirit-mind-*prana*-body and all of the mechanisms by which these four interact. (When I use the word *"prana,"* I am referring to the life force, which we take in as breath.) It also takes into account the relationship between personalities—in other words, the systems that constitute families, societies, nations, traditions, and all manner of small and large social units.

A Change of View

But what does all of this have to do with the words of Chanakya that were quoted earlier? Remember his maxim: "One who has conquered the self finds all his purposes and goals being accomplished."

Why is this so? Because meditation changes the way the mind looks at the world and interacts with it. What are all those thoughts and emotions constantly arising in your mind, anyway? They are simply conditioning. When you came into being in this lifetime, you had only awareness—and within that awareness, you had infinite potential. Then you were told many things: your name, your gender, your religion, your family history, and your national traditions. You were told all the things you could and couldn't do, and all the ways you should or shouldn't be. These identifications and expectations have determined how you look at and react to the world. But what if you were to look at the world once again from a place of pure awareness. This is the meditative perspective. From this perspective, you can observe your "self" functioning in the world; and from this perspective, you can govern that self.

Even in a basic beginner's exercise we see:

1. Awareness of breath replaces the arising of random sentiments and negative emotions,
2. Awareness of a word or sound flowing in the mind with the breath replaces random thoughts.

The first of these techniques—simple breath awareness—frees you to interpret the world with a more positive perspective. This brings a more positive response from others. As a result of this, your marriage or your parenting or your business deal proceeds more smoothly. After a while, the constant self-observation that comprises breath awareness makes you irresistible to others, who think of you in friendlier, more favorable terms. To use the ancient terminology, breath awareness helps you develop *ahimsa,* which means nonviolence. It also helps develop *maitri,* which means friendliness toward all beings, and which itself consists of *karuna* (compassion and empathy), *mudita* (joyfulness at others' progress as they become more virtuous people), and *upekkha* (indifferences to the weaknesses and failures of others).

How exactly do these things happen? On a manifest level, they happen through the mechanism of brain wave activity. Breath awareness, coupled with methodical relaxation exercises, changes the common beta brain wave pattern into an alpha pattern. The dominance of alpha waves provokes a nonviolent response to a situation that might otherwise provoke verbal, physical, or mental violence—the latter leading a person to malicious attitudes that can destroy harmony within a family, a community, or a business establishment. As for the awareness of a sound or word flowing in the mind with the breath, this leads to theta brain wave activity, which will help practitioners concentrate.

The second technique, the use of a single verbal thought flowing with the breath, helps with concentration, not only on a specific task in the moment but in the overall patterns of life. This technique generates theta brain waves that correlate with imagination and inventive creativity.

All of these things have practical consequences. Try to get even 5 percent of the people in a company meditating and see the "human resources" invariably improve dramatically within three to six months. Even with that small number meditating, see the productivity of the entire establishment rise within the same time frame.

You may have heard that a twenty-minute afternoon siesta helps with concentration and productivity of workers. The Himalayan system teaches that even more effective are frequent two-minute breath awareness breaks (even less time-consuming)!

Many years ago, when I was living in the USA, I received a call from a meditation student I had not seen in many years. He was now the president of a large trade union. He said he was calling to thank me, so I asked, "For what?" He said, "My union was on the verge of a strike. For the past week, the atmosphere was very hard, confrontational, and angry. I remembered your advice from the meditation classes. In the meeting rooms, where the atmosphere was very tense, I counted my breaths for two to five minutes. Every time I did this, I came out with a fresh proposal. Finally my proposals were accepted and yesterday we were able to avert the strike that would have adversely affected everyone in the state. So I have called to thank you."

Look how much comfort and happiness can be rooted in the peace of mind and the fresh perspective achieved through meditation. Notice how meditation generates not merely some otherworldly mystical state, but shows its effect with great success in down-to-earth affairs of politics and economics.

Meditation can positively impact material prosperity, which is, after all, the means of living. Allow me to give another example. Up to the end of the seventeenth century, India had one of the most successful economies in the world. That is why, when the Ottoman Empire blocked Europe's trade routes to India, there was such a concentrated endeavor to find new routes to that part of the world (leading, among other things, to the discovery of America). By the seventeenth century, India was producing almost 25 percent of the world's goods, and its currency was one of the strongest of its time. Today, some sixty-five years after achieving its independence from the British Empire, India is on the verge of recovering her ancient economic strength. I believe this is because of the personality traits and positive attitudes that the meditative tradition generates.

What all this shows is that we need not limit ourselves to scientific studies done in research laboratories to show the efficacy of meditation. We can look to the economic history of the world, in which the last two centuries of the West's economic dominance have been but a tiny fragment. History shows the effectiveness and success of the societies in which meditation and, more so, meditative attitudes have been the basis of civilization.

Just as Asia has taken up the West's computers, the East must take up Asia's meditation—not just as a twenty-minute-a-day technique, but also as the basis for positive relationships within business and society. Asia has taken the best of the West and retained the best of the East. Let the West retain the best of the West and take up the best of the East to ensure the continuity of its success.

Two

Speaking from Silence: The Art of Sensitive Communication

As we know, it can be difficult at first to quiet the mind in meditation, and it takes a bit of practice to get the hang of it. If you stick with it, however, you will find it becomes a very positive habit. Even so, the equanimity you find in meditation can be quickly shattered as soon as you come out of your solitude and converse with others. In such cases, who is it that is shattering that peace of mind you have so patiently cultivated?

Your spouse? Your neighbor? Your boss? Your client?

No, no, no, and no.

The one shattering your calm and centeredness is you—and you alone. You are responsible for your state of mind, but it is only once you begin to master the art of sensitive communication that you will be able to maintain it once you leave your meditation mat.

Who am I to be telling you about communication? It seems ironic, doesn't it? After all, as I mentioned, I recently began a five-year period of silence. Can a silent person teach others how to communicate? Perhaps a silent person is the best trainer for this purpose—for my tradition long ago began teaching the art of speaking from silence.

When I say "speaking from silence," I mean speaking from a place of calm, balance, neutrality, and nonreactivity, which is your true nature. When you communicate from such a state, you cannot be anything but sensitive to others. Sensitive communication is a very fine art, rooted in deep spiritual philosophies, but it also has very practical applications. For example, those who practice it are apt to find that their relationships improve, that their businesses prosper, that their leadership skills are enhanced, and that they are becoming the sort of people to whom it is very hard to say "no."

Sensitive communication cannot be learned in a day; however, in this chapter, I humbly offer you some principles on which to build your practice of "speaking from silence."

The Test of Three

Speaking from silence, or speaking from your true Self, requires speaking consciously and thoughtfully. It also requires exercising what is known as *sankalpa,* that is, the spiritual willpower that meditation can help you develop. It is all too easy to blurt out a string of words that expresses your visceral emotions and immediate reactions to people and situations. But how many times have you had the experience of wanting to take back your words or "bite your tongue" because what you have said is thought-less or hurtful or, at the very least, counterproductive? If you are like most people, you have had this experience many times. You know that once words have passed your lips, you have rung a bell that cannot be un-rung.

So I am going to pass on to you the three criteria that my tradition suggests a speaker or writer apply to any communication. We say that each spoken or written communication should be *hitam, mitam, pri-yam*—that is, beneficial, measured, and pleasant.

Now this might sound simple enough, and perhaps not too difficult to put into practice at, say, a garden party, where you are on your best be-havior, or a job interview for which you have rehearsed. But *hitam, mitam, priyam* are less easy for most of us to maintain when we are in potentially frustrating, trying situations. Can your words be beneficial (that is, helpful and constructive) when you are speaking to a repairman who is late, a customer service representative who cannot quickly resolve your complaint, or a coworker or subordinate who has missed an important deadline? Can your message be measured (that is, can you say just enough and no more) in such situations, or will you tend to run on and repeat yourself? Will the words you choose be harmless, or will they be harsh?

What about your tone? Do not underestimate the power of tone. Disagreements are generated not as often by differences on policies as they are by the tone of a communication. Can you modulate your voice and free it from the sound of anger or sarcasm?

You would be unusual, indeed, if you could do all of these things immediately upon making up your mind to do so. But if you make up your mind to practice the Test of Three much as you have made up your mind to practice meditation, eventually your communications will evolve. You will round off the sharp corners of your words—circle your word squares, as I like to say—and change harsh tones to pleasing tunes.

One way you can begin to practice is simply to slow down. A conversation is not a competition or a race. There is not a thing wrong with taking a few moments to consider your words.

Another way to practice is to remember to always smile before you speak. It is all right if you do not feel like smiling: smile, anyway. The same is true even if you are writing your words in a letter or e-mail and the other party will not see your smile. The smile is for you more than for them. It is difficult to be disagreeable with a smile on your lips. With the corners of your mouth upturned, you will find it easier to make *hitam, mitam, priyam* a habit.

Nonreactivity

But now you will ask, "What if the person I am speaking with is being rude to me? What if *he* is thoughtless? What if *she* is confrontational?"

And I ask you, "What of it?" Can you control another person? Of course not. The only thing you can control is the way you respond to that other person.

In the Himalayan tradition, we are seekers of *svatantrya,* or what you might call "nonreactivity." There is no exact English equivalent of this word, but it is roughly translated as "free volition coming from the voice of one's one soul or spiritual Self as opposed to conditioning." Perhaps the very best translation would be "true freedom." Think about the sense of independence you would experience if your actions and thoughts did not arise as reactions to situations and to others' actions. You would not be reactive, but instead independently active.

Being nonreactive, however, is a true challenge—not just on an emotional level but also on a physiological one. That is because we are actually wired to be reactive. A self-observant person will notice that quite often in a discussion, we register and begin to mimic even minor changes in the voice, tone, facial expressions, gestures, and body language of the person with whom we are speaking. They yawn; we yawn. They laugh; we laugh. This is due to what scientists have termed "mirror neurons"—brain cells that fire equally as enthusiastically when we perform an action as when we perceive someone else performing an action. Mirror neurons help us learn, and help us understand another's intentions. But they can also lead to emotional contagion. We can "catch" a bad mood from someone else. Our coworker frowns; we frown. Our frown makes us feel bad; they feel bad too. A negative feedback loop is established. Of course we can "catch" a good mood too. But do we really want to be at the mercy of other people's moods at all?

Proficient meditators, centered in stillness, can choose their feelings and emotions independently and not as an act of their mirror neurons. The methods for doing so have been taught by the ancients for thousands of years. As soon as the emotional state of another begins to reflect in us, we dive into our inner resources of relaxation and tranquility and thereby change the tone of the conversation.

On a practical level, the technique is relatively simple: The minute you observe a wrinkle developing, or a shadow of negativity passing over the face of someone you are speaking with, take remedial action by changing *your* emotional state of mind and thereby your tone of voice, gestures, and body language until all the wrinkles disappear. The opposite party's mirror neurons then reflect your state of mind, and both parties become peaceful and nonconfrontational.

I must mention it has also been said that mirror neurons are the source of empathy. Certainly, I am not advocating against empathy. In my language, one of the words for "compassion" and "empathy" is *anukampaa,* which literally means "trembling and vibrating with someone"—as when a *sitar* player plays that instrument's main strings and its sympathetic strings vibrate. Empathic listening and communicating are essential. But in my experience, there is a great difference between mimicry and empathy. When you encounter something disagreeable in someone, place your mind and heart in the place where that person is coming from. Take into account their background, culture, and psychology. In this context, you can address their concerns, but not condemn them. Then explain calmly the reasons for the actions you are taking.

Disagreements are, of course, inevitable from time to time. But they are no reason to abandon your resolve to communicate with sensitivity and to use words in a way that is beneficial, measured, and pleasant. A few ground rules:

- In all disagreements, first argue in your own mind in a direction opposite of your view. Ask yourself, *Is there a harmonious conjunction reflecting the best aspects of both?* The truth is that at the deepest level, there are no contradictory forces in the universe. All forces are complementary manifestations of the whole.
- Do not challenge or condemn a view without presenting a well-constructed alternative.

- Hold nothing in your mind against anyone. The moment a situation is complete, let your mind go neutral with a few deep breaths, and remember the good qualities of the other person.
- If you witness a disagreement between two parties, stay neutral. Do not become reactive in favor of one or another.

Perhaps the most important thing to remember about nonreactivity is that it requires taking complete responsibility for the ways in which *you* interact with others. You can no longer blame people for "making" you angry or causing you to say "things you did not mean." You must always look within for your direction, while treating others with respect.

To sum it up: If you have a problem with someone, solve the problem they have with you.

Be a "Yes Man" or "Yes Woman"

Some of you may wonder if adopting these methods of sensitive communication means you will not be able to make your ideas understood. Don't worry: It is always possible to communicate what you need to communicate. It is simply a question of how you say it. One thing that is best to avoid is negativity.

At my ashram, we have signs around the grounds that read: PLEASE LET THE FLOWERS BLOOM. Notice that the signs do not say: DO NOT PICK THE FLOWERS. The meaning of the two messages is the same, but the first is phrased positively, while the second is a prohibition—almost a reprimand.

Throughout history, philosophers and sages have urged us to conquer base emotions and strive to be close to Divine attributes. But in the contemporary West (and even sometimes in modern India, to my dismay), confrontational behavior is often encouraged in the name of "honest communication." If you feel put-upon, if you feel misunderstood, if you feel something is unfair, you look everybody in the eye and say a loud NO. But I come from a school of YES men, who think the best defense is nondefense. That is why hardly anyone says "no" to me.

Why say something straight if it can be curved? Curved by philosophy, curved by poetry, curved so as to reconcile differences. As in a circle, so the beginning becomes the end as opposites merge.

For example, someone asks you to approve a project for which it is not the right time or for which you do not have the resources. Instead of saying, "I will not approve it," try this: "If there were a possibility that this could be done, we would do it, but at this time the possibility looks very remote." In this type of communication, you have accomplished two very important goals:

1. You have made your position understood.
2. You have saved the other party's honor.

This type of communication is far more common in Eastern societies than in the West. For example, I was recently checking out of an Asian hotel, but planned to return there for a second stay within a few days. I asked, "May I pay all the bills at the end of my second stay, or should I settle the first one now?" The receptionist replied, "You may choose to pay now or when you come back. For us, it would be easier if you paid for each visit separately." I understood that she preferred me to pay then, and so I did.

Similarly, in an Asian country, one might ask a colleague, "May we hold a meeting at your home?" Answer: "My wife is away, but it would be a great pleasure for me to try to arrange the meeting at our home." The next day, you call him: "We are so grateful for your kind offer to host us. You are always so generous. For this time, another colleague has asked to be given a chance to host. Would it be all right with you if we accept?" Now everyone is content.

It requires a sensitivity of soul and heart to communicate this way. And it takes some getting used to. At first, it can even be a little confusing. I have known Western businessmen who visit Japan and leave not sure whether they have closed a deal or not. It could be said in such instances that one has to listen between the lines. Walk through a typical vegetable market in Asia, whether populated by Hindus, Buddhists, or Muslims, and you will likely hear a conversation that goes something like this:

"You do not have any fresh cabbage today?"

"Yes, sir."

Here the meaning of "Yes, sir" is "Yes, it is true we do not." Notice how no one has said "no."

These who come from more assertive cultures may not at first comprehend cultures where sensitive "curved" communication is the norm. But think how many misunderstandings, disputes, and perhaps even wars could be avoided if they did.

Why be an adversary if you don't have to be? The universe will serve to us what we pour into the universe. Say "yes" to the universe and the universe will say "yes" to you.

Sensitive Leadership

You may wonder if you can practice sensitive communication as a leader. In such a role, mustn't you clearly tell people what to do? Shouldn't sensitivity take a backseat?

Leaders, as much as anyone—perhaps more so than anyone else—must also practice *hitam, mitam, priyam*. Kindliness, self-observation, and self-control on the part of the leaders and guides ensure the highest possible functioning of the organization. Only a self-controlled leader maintains control. Only in the presence of a self-disciplined leader does an organization remain disciplined. Only in the presence of a humble leader or guide do others speak and behave humbly.

Leaders will do well to remember that they are first among equals, and that true loyalty cannot be demanded, but only earned. Sensitive communication is the best way to ensure that others will follow where you lead.

And so, if I may humbly suggest some guidelines for leaders and for those who would be leaders:

- No communication should be undertaken merely to impress on the "lower ranks" that "I am the boss here."
- Confer honors on others without seeking to be honored.
- Share with others all information that can safely be shared.
- Check how many sentences in your e-mails begin with the pronoun "I." Reduce the incidence of "I."
- Rather than saying, "Do it this way," ask, instead, "What would be the difficulties from your point of view if we did it this way?"
- Avoid words like "no," "not," "reject," "forbid," and "deny."
- Remember that if the listener does not understand your intent, the flaw is in you. Try again.

The aim of all of these practices is to let others feel that they are leading and that you are merely suggesting. In such a way, you will create the most cohesive of teams. However, you will notice that if you are to be successful in such an endeavor, you must be willing to give your ego a rest and let your true Self come to the fore.

The true Self is humble. But remember that humility toward superiors is no humility at all. Rather, it is a humble attitude toward those *you lead* that will be the secret to your success.

Leaders, be ambitious! Aspire to be the most humble of God's creatures and thereby share in God's grandeur.

Three

PROGRESS AND ROADBLOCKS

The spiritual path is like any other path in that there are signposts along the way to show you that you are making progress. If you are not only practicing your meditation, but also letting that meditation guide you toward calmer, more satisfying interactions with others, then you should notice a few "signposts":

You will be able to find the positive concealed in the negative.

You will decondition the mind from its habits, to free it from running in preset grooves.

You will free the mind from the habit of being in conflict and learn to resolve potential conflicts before they erupt.

You will develop fresh insights of a positive nature into relationships, communications, and events and apply these.

You will glean insights into philosophical realities and truths.

On a practical level, you will experience fewer problems in daily life. If some problems do arise, they will fail to create depression or anxiety. In the absence of such debilitating emotions, you will have a clear, undisturbed mind in which spontaneous solutions arise, showing you shortcuts to your goals.

How to Stay on the Path

If you are facing problems, figure out where your spiritual progress is lacking. Remind yourself to do the following:

- Keep daily meditation. It will grant you insight and verify the factualness of what is presented in these pages.
- Keep your forehead relaxed—free of the wrinkles of worry and repetitive thought—in all situations. (This sounds easier than it is—but keep trying!)
- Every two to three hours, do two to three minutes of breath awareness with a mantra. (Do this sitting, standing, even with your eyes open while in a meeting, if you need to.) Just keep doing it—it will change your temperament.
- Observe yourself constantly. Take note every time you have not quite managed to remain true to your principles of speech and behavior. (Ask yourself: *Was there a touch of unnecessary harshness in my tone? Did I neglect to practice non-anger or humility?*)
- Use your *sankalpa*—your spiritual willpower. Resolve to do better next time, but do not indulge in self-condemnation. Never give up on yourself; just renew your *sankalpa*.
- Select one principle you find it easiest to practice and also one you find it most difficult to practice. Start practicing.
- Devise your own methods to apply these principles.

Are you doing all of these things?

As you continue to accrue successes in these practices, and as the practices reveal their benefits to you, remember them and let them serve as inspiration for the future. Take care not to let your successes become a source of pride (aspire to humility!), but at the same time allow them to fuel your continuation on the path.

When Destructive Emotions Arise

Just as you will know when you are making progress, you will know when you have encountered what seems to be a roadblock. You will know your progress is stalled when you experience a lack of fulfillment and general inner satisfaction— and when you experience a general emptiness and loneliness that you might try to fill not by nurturing your mind but by overfilling your stomach.

What are the culprits behind these unproductive states? They are destructive emotions such as greed, anger, and self-centeredness.

In the following chapters, I will talk more about emotions. It is important to understand them, for they are what will keep you centered and sensitive or, conversely, lead you astray.

But before we begin, let me offer this wish and blessing for you:

May you not become your emotions.
May your free will guide them.

Four

LET THE MIND READ THE MIND

How do you know if an emotion is good or bad? Better to ask: *Is this emotion in harmony with my urge to Self-create, to become a fuller person? Does it make me inclusive or exclusive?*

For example, let's say you experience the emotion of anger. By definition, it causes you to exclude someone. You say to someone with whom you are angry, "Get out of my life!" Then perhaps you feel satisfied for a fleeting moment.

But the catch is that exclusive emotions are self-defeating. The angrier you become with someone, the more strongly you think of him. It's illogical, because your obsessive thought doesn't fulfill the purpose of your anger, which was ostensibly to banish your nemesis. Now the "unwanted" person is always on your mind. You can't forget him! You must love him so much. . . . After all, you love the thought of him. And on some level you relish the torture that thought gives you. But why choose self-torture? Your exclusiveness is self-defeating.

The only way out of this conundrum is mindfulness. Observe your emotions; witness them. Let the mind read the mind. Through mindfulness, you watch an emotion and you recognize that it is there. Then you categorize it.

Types of Emotion

In our tradition, we ask, "Is an emotion *sattvic, rajastic,* or *tamasic?*"

Sattva refers to energy that is luminous, peaceful, harmonious, serene, gentle, intuitive, and light.

Rajas refers to energy that is active, progressive, and creative when serving *sattva*, or kinetic and restless when not serving *sattva*.

Tamas refers to energy that is stabilizing when serving *sattva,* or heavy, inert, and dark when not serving *sattva*.

If this is confusing at first, I will make it very simple. You have a feeling and the mind reads the mind and says, *Now I have this emotion. Is it harmonious? Is it productive? Is it calming? Or does it unsettle me or weigh me down?* Resolve that whatever centers you, you will follow, and that what scatters you, you will not follow.

Will doing this make you a moral person? Of course! For morality has no other definition. If we were all to examine emotions in this manner, our acts would automatically become unselfish and inclusive. It is only when true spirituality is excluded from our lives that morality must be enforced by outside forces. But when that is the case, no matter how many police we train or armies we raise, we will all be less safe.

The Components of an Emotion

Once you observe your own emotions, you will also be able to begin to clearly and objectively analyze the emotions of others. Furthermore, you can analyze the components of each emotion. Where is it coming from? What are its component parts? What has led to it? What are the forces behind it? The mind takes many things from many sources and integrates them, assimilates them, and creates a hodgepodge of something new. But consider its sources.

For example, let's say I am walking down the street in America, on my way to my meditation center, and I am wearing the traditional orange wraparound garb of a swami. Someone may give me a glance that looks angry, suspicious, and anxious. Maybe he thinks I am a follower of some strange witchcraft religion. I don't look like a minister or a priest. What is this, a cult? He believes in Jesus. He assumes I do not believe in Jesus. (Never mind that Jesus never wore pants and a shirt!) And to top it off, maybe I am from a poor country whose immigrants cannot wait to overrun his country. The trouble is that I just do not fit into this person's existing patterns. All that buildup from his past has been concentrated in this one angry glance at me.

But I do not get angry in return. Because I have this analytical habit, I watch that glance of his and I am very interested. I recognize that what I am wearing is not what he saw men of religion wear in his childhood. I also know he did not choose his emotion. He did not pay attention in that micro-millionth of a second where the assertion of his will could have intervened. His nerves are weak after a long day of work, and all day long he has not breathed properly. There is tension in him that is waiting for some stimulus to create a response, and it just so happens that I am in his line of sight. I know I am not really the object of his anger at all.

I think, *Okay. If he did not have me to oppose, he would have somebody else. I am not going to harm him, whereas that somebody else might harm him.* You see, once you understand the forces behind an emotion, you will not react in the familiar way. No more anger for anger; no more eye for an eye.

Personality and Karma

Emotions can be hard to manage because they have built up habits in the mind over one's entire lifetime. In fact, what I truly believe is that emotions go even deeper than that. I believe that God creates and dissolves the world again and again, and that we are born and die and are born again and again . . . until we fully merge our individual will with the Divine will.

We have gathered the force of *karma* in this process of reincarnation. What is the force of karma? It is the sum total of the residue that I have gathered in my mind—not only in this lifetime, but also from previous lives.

Even if you do not believe in reincarnation, that need not change how you begin to deal with your emotions. Let's say you have been gathering momentum in your mind since the moment of birth in this lifetime, or since the moment of conception in this lifetime. No matter. Momentum has still been gathered. Some of us have passed through a thick cloud of dust, while some have passed through a thin layer of dust. The thicker the layer of dust—that is, the thicker the brew of emotions—the less Divine light filters through. But in the micro-moment it takes to realize that all of the things I'm doing are being done out of momentum the mind has given itself by gathering residues and impressions and karmas—in that moment I can say to myself, *No, thank you. Not for me. I am going to step off this treadmill and break the cycle.*

And if I can't completely extinguish all of these feelings burning in my mind, then once a day, or twice a day, I'm going to calm them down by meditating. Slowly I'm going to increase my period of calm. I'm going to sweep off the layer of dust that has gathered on my mind, little by little by little.

Analyze the Feeling, Not the Situation

People often raise an objection to examining their feelings, and it goes something like this: "*Of course* I'm upset that somebody said and did this to me! You're telling me not to be upset. Are you so holy and sanctimonious that you *wouldn't* be upset if this happened to you?"

We feel like this so often because we are talking about a situation and our reaction to the situation, but we are not analyzing our reaction itself. Remember, the goal is to be nonreactive, for that is the only path to true freedom. So, if a feeling arises that seems irresistible, we must more than ever ask ourselves:

- Where is it coming from?
- Why am I acting this way?
- What is it that I am resisting?

We think, *That person—he's just terrible, he's bad, and that's why I'm resisting him.* But this is not true. Ask him. He'll contradict you immediately. Now you have your word and you have his word.

So, even if you run away from this person, or knock him unconscious, here you are and you have to deal with yourself. You have to inquire, *What are the contents of this load of emotion? What past residue is attached to it? What association?* And finally, *Is my reaction going to make me an inclusive person or an exclusive person?*

It is amazing what happens when someone consciously decides not to react in a preprogrammed way. I remember long ago when my wife was raising our four small children while I was often off teaching and lecturing. Once, we had a disagreement. I wrote her a nasty note, left it on her desk, and went somewhere. I returned to my desk in the evening and found a beautiful little bird made of decorated stone. There was no reply to my note. I didn't even remember what the problem was. All I knew then, and all I recall now, is that I left a nasty note and I found this beautiful gift. I won't say we dealt with our problems so perfectly all the time, but I can tell you that meditation helped.

So often we neglect to use our will. We have reactions and jumbled impulses and we think these represent our free choice. But how fragile we really are if we are in a reactive stance. Who are "you" if someone asks a simple question and you feel threatened? If you were behaving rationally, you would not be so aggressive, so defensive. A person who lives in fulfillment within his true Self does not become defensive. In fact, 80 percent of the time such a person will naturally say, "Yes, you are right. I hear you. It's okay."

What is the point in hurting another person just to protect your ego? Let me tell you a story. There once was an emperor in India who was such a beautiful person that he would not take anything for himself from the royal treasury. His treasury was for the benefit of the people. So the emperor made his living by copying manuscripts, becoming very famous for both his intellect and his artistic calligraphy. One day a scholar walked into his court. You have probably met people who come into your room and start leafing through your papers. Just so, the scholar started looking through the emperor's papers and said, "Your Majesty, this passage is not correct. It should be like this." The emperor said, "Oh, yes," and he picked up his correcting fluid, crossed off what he had written, and made the correction the scholar noted. The scholar was very happy. After partaking of the emperor's hospitality, he returned home and told others, "The emperor is a very nice man; he listens to scholars." Meanwhile, the emperor picked up the correcting fluid again and replaced the previous wording because he knew he had been right in the first place. "But," he asked, "why hurt the feelings of a scholar?"

The East/West Idea of Mind

I have said, "Let the mind read the mind." But to make this clearer, let me tell you what I mean by "mind." In the Western system of psychology, mind is more or less a process. There is no definition of the word "mind" in any psychology textbook. But Eastern psychology has a definite definition of mind. It is a particular type of energy. By this, I don't mean "kinetic energy," as in "feeling energetic." Think of the way in which you imagine energy as light, energy as heat, electricity, magnetism, gravity, and so on. These are very defined and refined forms of energy, which go through different types of oscillations, which are measured as voltage, wattage, and so many amperes. If the energy in your battery is weak, the engine won't start. If your house only has so much voltage and you plug in too many appliances, your circuits blow out.

Think of the mind as a field of something real—definitive, measurable energy—that can be increased like voltage and decreased like voltage, that can be increased like light and decreased like light. What is the difference between weak light and strong light? The answer is energy flow. You can increase it or decrease it. All emotional, neurotic, psychotic, creative, and relational actions, experiences, and symptoms—*everything* depends on the strength of your mind.

Consider the symptoms of what happens when the mind field is weak versus when it is strong. Many people think that a strong, open flow of emotional expression—a blowup—exhibits strength of mind. But if you plug six appliances into one socket and the circuit blows out, does that show the strength of the field of electricity behind it? A blowup is not a symptom of strength; it's a symptom of weakness in the energy field. The proper measure of strength is a flow of energy that can sustain these appliances and keep them functioning at an even pace. Likewise, a strong mind is measured by its constancy and evenness.

The mind is connected to the world of phenomena, people, and relationships through the channels of the senses, nerves, and brain. That is why, for example, we say we see the color "blue" when in fact there is no such thing as "blue," but rather a particular wavelength of light that strikes the eye and creates a physiological and, in turn, a cognitive reaction. We can all agree on this, and we think that is all there is to know about the mind. But there is something beyond the mind from which the mind draws its power and strength. So, what and where is that powerhouse from which the mind can manage a million things and not "blow out"? The source is the life force itself—which my tradition calls the *"kundalini"*—and its power can be channeled through concentration. This is where meditation comes in.

Meditation is derived from the Latin *medi*, which means the "center" or "middle," and *tare,* which means "to stay." To come to the center within you and stay there—this is meditation; this is concentration. Centering is the powerful aspect of meditation. As you focus the mind within itself, you find a gateway to the freedom of will.

We sell ourselves short when we think the mind is merely a compendium of anything and everything we absorb, like impressions and memories. We are mistaken when we think only the things we see become part of our mind. Then, if I react to what I see, I say I am "speaking my mind." We have not realized that the power of mind comes from something greater, and so we have blocked the source of the mind's real energy. Because of this blockage, the poor mind is starved. The only nourishment it can depend on is what it is being fed from outside rather than from within. Your mind is living on take-out food!

When we sit and meditate, we recharge our batteries from a source within ourselves. That is one way to connect to the energy field of the mind. A second way is by practicing mindfulness as we go about our day. This keeps the mind's generator going—since it cannot run on battery power alone.

We can practice mindfulness by maintaining an awareness of something at the center of the mind, such as a mantra, as we go about our lives. We can also practice it by letting the mind read the mind.

How often we wish we had the power to read other people's minds! Well, why don't we begin with our own? Make it your business to know what is going on in your mind twenty-four hours a day. This is not as daunting a task as it may sound. Each time the mind thinks a thought, the higher part of the mind is aware that a thought is being processed. You simply observe. Are you in the habit of thinking destructive thoughts? Watch. Now say to yourself, *Here comes that destructive thought again. What good is it doing me? Good-bye!* In that micro-millionth of a second, your free will comes to the surface and decides, *Mind, think this thought; do not think that thought.*

Because of all that you have deposited in your mind and because of the momentum you have given it, the part of your mind that is habituated to a familiar thought will throw a tantrum at first—like a young child who is told he must wait until later for something he wants. But after a number of tantrums, the resistance will diminish.

There are many parts of the mind. One part runs all your body's automatic systems—breathing, digestion, and so on. Another processes our sensory perceptions—what we see and hear and taste. Yet another part of the mind chews its cud, watching the interplay of all the residue of past accumulations all the time—first unconsciously, but then consciously, with practice.

But the primary part of the mind is its connection with free will. This is where it is at its purest and most beautiful. This part is realized when the mind recognizes the one consciousness that is the life force. Having recognized that force, the mind becomes resonant with light. If the light and the sound of the universe become one, and you can listen to it for twelve hours a day out of twenty-four, you are no longer an ordinary human being. If you can listen to it one out of every twenty-four hours, you are a saint. Aim high. Aim for sainthood! If you do not get there in this lifetime, you will still have improved your life beyond measure.

Five

THE CREATIVE POWER OF EMOTIONS

Analyzing and managing your emotions is a good beginning, but as you go further, another worthwhile goal is to refine your emotions. That is, turn the grosser emotions into finer ones. If you do this, you will automatically become, among other things, a more creative person.

What do I mean by "creativity"? The act of creating an object such as a painting, poem, or sculpture is one kind of creativity. Creating something in another person is a second kind. But creating something of oneself is the highest form of creativity.

If I make beautiful paintings or write beautiful verses, what good is it if my mind curses all the time? We say that painting and poetry are fine arts, but are they the finest? Better to create out of yourself a beautiful and lovable person—one whose presence can create a smile where there were tears. You can accomplish this only if you know how to use emotions creatively, transforming *tamasic* qualities into *rajastic* ones, and *rajastic* qualities into *sattvic* ones. That is truly the finest art of all.

It is only when you have created something beautiful in yourself that you can then also create something beautiful in another. You can take your worst opponent and turn him into your best friend if you know how to use your emotions creatively—because then you can also use your opponent's emotions creatively.

Creating refined *sattvic* emotions in yourself reminds you that you must build relationships on the basis of being a complete, whole person—not a part. When you discuss a disagreement over an issue with someone, it should not color your entire life. Imagine tempers are rising; but in the middle of that hot dispute, you suddenly create a change. You shift ground. You get up and bring a glass of water for each of you. You take a sip; you let your "adversary" take a sip. The whole mood changes. Carry on then with your disagreement, having made the point that your entire relationship is not colored by this one little dispute.

Even if the other person will not accept a sip of water from you, it's okay. He might not take it this time; but if you accept that, then your very acceptance of his refusal is a constructive act. As a result of this—slowly, slowly—some of the hostility in the interpersonal atmosphere begins to evaporate. The particular issue you are arguing about may or may not be resolved. It doesn't matter—because the main thing is that it no longer colors your entire relationship.

I am aware that there is a lot of advice that contradicts my own. Why not stare your opponent down? Why not one-up him? Why not play whatever power games you can play? I'll tell you why: Because then you might seem to have external success, but your Self-creativity will be destroyed.

Maybe you think it's okay to play a power game with a coworker or business associate. But how long, then, before you play it with your wife, your husband, your children? If you train your mind to play power games at work for eight hours a day, you can't possibly come home with a pure and loving mind. You will play the same games at home. Is that what you want?

Can You Do What You Don't Like Doing?

As you have gathered, I believe in promoting consensus rather than confrontation. But if you are going to give up the need to "win" every disagreement, doesn't that mean that sometimes you are going to have to do what you do not want to do? Yes! And so what?

You have to cultivate emotional strength. To be able to do what you don't want to do requires a strong mind. A human being can do things he does not like and do them successfully if he is in a situation from which running away at this stage of life would mean destroying something else, somewhere else. Such is the case with the salesman who does not like the methods his company uses to sell products, but he has a family and another child on the way. Such is the case with the student who must forgo social life to study for exams.

Then there are cases where we are not pleased with some of the ongoing circumstances of our lives, but still we must persevere. There is the woman or the man who wanted to marry years ago and has never met the right person. Each time this man and woman try their hand at love and fail, they lose more confidence. Should they stop trying to find a husband or wife? If they have strong minds, they will have shock absorbers to absorb disappointment and to prevent them from developing a loss of confidence. Should they throw a tantrum? Maybe that's okay, but only if the tantrum subsides quickly. We think of children as being emotionally weak because they throw tantrums. However, immediately after throwing their tantrum, it's as if they have no memory of it. They can come and hug their parent and smile sweetly, bearing absolutely no malice—because the purity of mind that exists in childhood keeps their shock absorbers lubricated and in good working order. Sadly, we become stiff as we grow older. We have fewer shock absorbers, unless we deliberately cultivate them.

What I'm suggesting with these examples once again is that you consider the whole and not let parts of your life affect your entire personality. If your shock absorbers are working correctly, you can look at any situation from a *sattvic* perspective, a refined intellect. You tell yourself that an unpleasant part of a job is not a whole job, and a job is not your whole life. And so there is no reason to come home and take things out on your spouse, your children, or your other relationships.

By keeping your mind strong, you can also switch gears very easily. You can shake off the effects of a "bad day." Instead of grinding your gears until they cease to function, you shift effortlessly from one circumstance to another. You have to keep your shock absorbers and your gears greased, and daily lubrication is provided by your breathing, by your meditation, and by centering yourself with your concentration.

If you are truly devoted to refining your thoughts and emotions, you will find that you will become so skillful at adapting to circumstances that the circumstances themselves may appear to alter. Swami Rama, my own guru, told a story about a time in the eighteenth and nineteenth centuries when many humanistic thinkers—like Voltaire, Thomas Paine, Mark Twain, Darwin, and Tolstoy—were condemned to Hell by the bishops of their time. Well, when a bishop condemns you to Hell, you have no choice: You go to Hell!

Being holy, the bishops themselves went to Heaven, of course. One day in the far future, they decided to pay their fallen opponents a visit, expecting to find that the humanists and scientists would be baking and suffering. But in Hell the bishops found no terrible heat or flames, no cries of anguish. Instead, there were flowers, trees, canals, and many beautiful respites.

"What happened to Hell?" asked the bishops. "What's this place here?"

"Why, this is Hell," said the fallen ones. "We were condemned to a place called Hell, but we believed in our own humanity and science and creativity. You had a ready-made Heaven; but since we did not have that good fortune, we put in air-conditioning, altered the climate, and built hothouses. We made our own little Heaven right here."

Obviously, the moral of the story is simple: If you find yourself in Hell, create your own Heaven right there.

From the Outside In

Another important thing to say about refining your emotions is that it is wise to start bit by bit. You may finish this chapter with great, holy intentions. However, when you put these pages aside, those pure intentions may begin to dissipate after five minutes.

You might drive down the road and a car will pass you too closely and you will want to curse. Or you may once again become caught up in destructive emotions related to a familiar person or a situation that you find frustrating. Remember, please, that this is only part of your life. Meanwhile, work on the other parts of your life where you do not have such difficulty with negativity. This does not make you a hypocrite; it does not make you a failure. It is perfectly reasonable to begin to do your work on the fringes, where things are not so extreme.

Once upon a time, in the fourth century BC, a man named Alexander of Macedonia—today known as Alexander the Great—invaded India. He tried to conquer the country, but Alexander's armies were eventually defeated by an Indian prince, Chandragupta Maurya. Later that prince waged a rebellion against the existing Indian emperor. He tried to raise a revolt right in the middle of the city, where the emperor reigned.

Failing, the prince went on the run, escaping into the mountains in disguise. It is said that as he walked alone, tired and hungry, he came upon the home of an old widow who gave him shelter for the night and prepared him a simple supper of rice and lentils. The dish was very hot; and since the woman did not have a spoon or fork to offer, the prince put his fingers right in the middle of the dish and burned himself.

The old woman looked at him, exclaiming, "You are just like that rebel prince!"

"Why, what did he do?" asked the prince, quite startled.

"He went and raised a rebellion right in the middle of the capital city. Is that any way to organize a rebellion? In your plate of hot rice, you should start eating from the sides. The sides cool first. You eat them and move slowly into the center. It is the same with that rebel. He should have started with the surrounding villages and countryside and then slowly closed in on the city."

The prince replied, "Madam, you are right. You are the greatest diplomat and politician I've ever met. No one ever taught me that!"

Later he organized his rebellion again just that way, becoming emperor himself.

The story may be apocryphal, but its lesson is invaluable. Test your strength slowly, on the peripheries, on those little areas that are easiest to handle. Work on those, and do not give up. The rest will follow in time.

Six

REJOICE WITHOUT REASON

In this chapter I am going to invite you to become a fool. "All right," you may think, "that will be easy!" But as you will see, it can really be quite a challenge—albeit with great rewards. But we will get to all of that in a little while. Right now, I want to ask you a question:

Who is responsible for your feelings?

When you have a feeling, you often ascribe it to another person, don't you? In fact, you often blame someone for the emotions you are experiencing. You say, "You made me feel guilty," or "You made me feel uncomfortable," or perhaps simply, "You hurt my feelings." When you say things like this, you are implying that there are right ways and wrong ways to feel—and that another person made you feel the "wrong" feelings. You are certainly ascribing a great deal of power to this other person.

But when you yourself have a feeling and act on it, you really don't think of that feeling in terms of whether it is right or wrong, do you? You say, "Of course I yelled. I was angry." You don't stop to question the anger. The anger seems like flowing water, or like burning fire: You see it as just an inevitable force.

But you can't have it both ways. You have to make a decision. Are there right and wrong feelings? And who controls the feelings that you have?

Feelings are mental activities. When you do not have a direct, rational "cause and effect" associated with something—but rather you have indirect associations—you create a thought that is called a "feeling." Instead of thinking, you emote. Your urges, your mental habits, your conscious and unconscious associations, your pleasant and unpleasant memories, and even your impressions from past lives (what my tradition calls "samskaras") all create feelings for you. Then you believe you are helpless.

But I contend that there *are* right and wrong feelings, and you can recognize them and choose between them. I also contend that you are never truly helpless in the face of feelings. Your feelings are *your* responsibility—and yours alone. And it is up to you to steer yourself in the direction of good, uplifting emotions and to draw your attention away from destructive ones.

You ask yourself: *How can I choose my emotions? My emotions just appear!* Well, sometimes you are driving down the road and a ditch appears. Do you have to drive into it?

Remember once again that as a meditator you are striving constantly to purify your mind so that your personality may also be purified and so that the barrier between you and the Divine gradually thins, diminishes, and vanishes. Without the purification of your emotions, you will never come face-to-face with the great transcendental reality. If transcendence is your goal, then purification of your feelings is not optional. It must be undertaken.

You need to decide the kind of feelings you want to cultivate in yourself, as well as those you want to avoid. Is it possible? Yes. Just as it is possible to withhold our hand when we feel the urge to strike in rage, it is ultimately possible to withhold that rage. It is within our power to curb absolutely any feeling at all.

Of course this process must be done step by step. Remember, we need to begin at the edges. First we must learn to recognize the presence of certain feelings as soon as they arise. Next we need to ask if each feeling is desirable or undesirable. Then we need to take responsibility for our feelings. Another person may be an excitant for them or a catalyst or a trigger—but the inherent quality is present in us. What are *we* going to do with it?

Maybe you feel attached to some of your negative, destructive thoughts: *My boss is mean. My spouse is manipulative. My mother makes me feel guilty.* Dwelling on them can become very addictive. It feels good to be so sure and so righteous, doesn't it? But only for a while.

Undesirable feelings have a way of boomeranging. If you throw a boomerang, it comes back and can hit you. And it becomes an even more powerful missile on its return journey. So examine your feelings not in relationship to others, but in relationship to yourself, instead. What is already in your makeup that these other people are illuminating? What wonderful teachers your "tormentors" are!

If you continually examine your emotions this way, eventually you will be capable of:

- Eliminating undesirable thoughts;
- Preventing undesirable thoughts from occurring in the first place;
- Causing desirable thoughts to arise;
- Maintaining all desirable thoughts that have arisen.

On Being a Fool

Now let's talk some more about desirable feelings. Maybe they are not as easy to recognize at first as undesirable ones. When you examine a feeling or aspiration, you should ask yourself, *Does this feeling lead me to a purer thought? Does it lead to a happy feeling within me, a rejoicing feeling?*

Rejoicing about what? you ask.

In my tradition, we say that rejoicing need not necessarily be *about* anything. A person who rejoices just rejoices. He sings for no reason at all. We've all had such moments. We practically skip down the street; we whistle a tune that comes "from nowhere." Now recognize those moments as your source of strength. Let them be your standard to measure against.

In the eyes of others, someone who is joyful without a reason may be a fool. But in the eyes of the Divine, he is a wise man. In fact, you can never really become a wise man unless you go through a period of looking like a fool in other people's eyes.

Now this doesn't mean that all foolish things are wise, so take care to discriminate. Once again, train yourself to recognize feelings, to examine them, to claim them as your own, and to recognize that they can be curbed.

Time Is Precious

Human life, human time, is very precious. It should not be thrown away on negative things. You've no business searching out and blaming the "culprit" who "gave" you a bad feeling. A bomb is about to explode. Somebody rushed by and handed that bomb to you and here you are questioning his motives. Does that help? Get rid of the bomb! Run! Move fast! Recognize the fact that *that feeling* is a bomb capable of destruction.

I earlier said we were aiming for complete nonreactivity. But for now, be selective in what you react to. React positively to positive things; seek out positive things to respond to. Is there even one small thing in an unhappy situation that makes you happy? Focus on that.

If two people are in the same circumstances—and one finds something positive and reacts positively, while one finds something negative and reacts negatively—we know that the fault is not in that circumstance.

The one reacting negatively has something negative within, which must be recognized. If I am that one, I must alter my feelings by training myself. And I can always, always ask for help. Knowing that the right feelings will lead me closer to the Divine, I ask, "God, please help me cultivate the right feelings."

And help is on its way.

Seven

A "Get Out of Jail Free" Card

Maybe you are thinking that, yes, you would like to have more joy in your life, but unfortunately you cannot right now. You cannot until you are free—free from . . . Fill in your own blank.

Free from money troubles?

Free from the ten extra pounds you have gained?

Free from your impossible boss?

Free from your nagging spouse?

Free from your demanding children?

We always attach a condition to freedom. We never just seek freedom, but rather seek freedom *from X*. In ordinary daily life, we are caught up in these limited, dependent concepts of freedom.

This sort of freedom, though, is not the kind imagined by Socrates, nor by Jesus and Buddha, nor by Lao-tze and the great philosophers of China, nor by the great yogis and masters of India. These great beings thought only of *absolute freedom:* freedom that is true and lasting because it is dependent on nothing.

If you think about it, you will see that the sort of freedom that is *from something* really just creates another kind of bondage. Let me offer a concrete example. Let's say I have an apartment, and I find it too small and confining. How I wish I were free from this oppressive little space! So I save and scheme and buy a house. Now I am a homeowner with so much to do because my house is so large. I have so many chores and expenses. I wish I were free of them. Maybe one day I will just rent a small apartment and downsize. How I wish to be free from the burden of my big house!

You know what happens after that? The cycle of bondage and of craving for release begins again. This applies to everything: to divorce, marriage, friends, enemies, employment, unemployment, and so on. Try to think abut freedom from any X-1 in your life that has not immediately brought about another condition of confinement imposed by X-2. And when you find freedom from X-2, there is the restraint of X-3 waiting for you. You may argue that it is better to be bound by certain things than others. It is better, to be sure, to be bound by the constraints of a recovery program than to be bound to alcohol, for example. Of course I agree. But although you are, in such a case, refining from a lower level to a higher level—and although this elevation is a positive thing—you are still not free in the absolute sense.

What Is Free Will?

The search for freedom is like un-nesting a set of Russian dolls. Remove the first one and there is another and another and another inside. This is because the moment you create a past, you create a future—in other words, this is the way of karma.

We often think we are making free choices, when, in fact, deep within our unconscious mind, our choices have already been made. Will I marry this one or that one? Will I become a doctor or an engineer or a monk? When I am released from prison, will I walk to the left or to the right? We think we are making these decisions, but the decisions are actually made—subjugated to the seeds of what has gone before.

Most of us are not aware that this is so. We have not realized that we are bound by our unconscious dictates—and so we are not aware that we can overcome the bondage to our unconscious mind. But I say that it can be done—and not just by a saint or a Buddha. I say even an average individual can do so.

True freedom is a question of volition. Volition is beyond the unconscious mind. But where is it? Is it in the conscious mind? No! The conscious mind is a slave of the unconscious mind. Of course the conscious mind does not know this—but the worst kind of slavery is when you do not realize that you are enslaved. You think you are acting under your own steam, but you are not.

True free will comes not from the mind but from the luminous current that powers the mind—and that itself can be accessed through meditation and *sankalpa* (spiritual willpower). In Chapter 5, I mentioned that the strong mind has emotional "shock absorbers" and that these allow us to look at any situation from a *sattvic* perspective—that is, from a perspective that is serene, harmonious, and truly intuitive. So, what if we were to access this current and operate from there?

Let's say you are feeling angry. You are a slave to that anger; it rules you day and night. You have three choices. The first is to be angry. The second is to repress anger. (For a while, this may masquerade as "freedom from anger," but, of course, it is not.) The third choice is not to be angry, and then there is no reason to repress anger. How do you go about making the third choice? You think you cannot help being angry, but I'm saying that you can. You cannot do it by fixing the person who is "making you angry." Remember, no one can make you angry *but you.*

Or let us say you are alone. This is an objective fact: Somewhere you are in a cabin all by yourself. In the same conditions, some people suffer more, some less, and some not at all. So, again, you have a choice of emotions: You can choose to suffer loneliness or you can choose to enjoy solitude. Here is where volition comes in. You can sit down and write letters decrying the suffering of your loneliness. On the other hand, if you happen to be Thoreau, you can write a book on the joys of Walden Pond.

Your anger and your loneliness are waves on the infinite sea. To go beyond them, you must dive deep into the sea—into the still, silent dimension from which all thoughts arise. But how? you ask. How do I distinguish what is coming from the unconscious from what is emanating from the inherent, absolute freedom and the self-luminous light that I am? The answer is a little complex, but please stay with me. If you do, I promise to stay right here with you.

The Five Causes of Suffering

What is coming from inherent and absolute freedom (rather than the freedom that is dependent upon bondage to something) is recognizable because it is not bound by the five causes of suffering, or what my tradition calls the five *"kleshas."*

The five *kleshas* are ignorance, ego, attachment, aversion, and fear of death.

Ignorance (*Avidya*)

The first discovery of the Buddha on attaining enlightenment was that the world was full of suffering, that suffering arises from craving, and that craving arises from *avidya* (ignorance). But in this case, "ignorance" is not the absence of intellectual information. Rather, it is a flaw in perspective. Examples of *avidya* include:

- Considering this world as eternal, even though it is finite;
- Considering the spirit as though it dies, even though it is eternal;
- Mistaking pure for impure, and impure for pure, in our conduct;
- Mistaking the pain of attachment for pleasure, and the pleasure of nonattachment for pain.

In short, all of these misperceptions are made because of mistaking the Self for non-self and non-self for Self. We think that when the body is born, we are born; or that when the body dies, we die. But this is not so. To paraphrase a critical passage from the *Bhagavad Gita*: As a man discards worn-out clothes and puts on new ones, likewise the embodied soul casting off worn-out bodies enters into others that are new. Weapons cannot cut the soul, nor can fire burn it. Water cannot drench it, nor can wind make it dry. For this being is impenetrable. It is eternal, omnipresent, immovable, constant, and everlasting. . . . Therefore, knowing this as such, you should not grieve.

Imagine if you could internalize the wisdom of this passage. That would be your answer to all painful and destructive emotion.

Ego (*Asmita*)

Often we say, "I am," and then attach our identity to an emotion. We say, "I am happy, sad, mad, glad, stressed, bored, falling in love, falling out of love." But, of course, the essence of our being is not to be equated with any of these states. They are just passing states, after all. I think anyone would agree with this.

But likewise, it is customary to define our "I-am-ness" in terms we consider more concrete: "I am a man, woman, doctor, lawyer, teacher, husband, wife"; "I am tall, short, fat, skinny"; "I am Italian, German, American, Chinese, African." But remember the words of the *Gita* and you will realize that these, too, are just passing states. They do not define our essence. Only *atman* (the soul) is our essence.

When we meet someone we want to know, who are *you*? But here we are also looking for superficialities. We want to know what we have in common with someone, and how we are different. But in the end, deep beneath the surface, all differences dissolve.

Of course we need an ego to function in the world and to relate to others. You are asked to introduce yourself at a dinner party. It is probably just as well that you do not declare, "I am the eternal, transcendent Reality." It is fair to say that this could be a conversation stopper. However, internally, it is when we forget the nature of the true Self and the fact that all beings are interconnected—not separate egos but, ultimately, one and the same—that we suffer.

Let me explain further. If you are in a room with me, you think you see me, right? And that I see you? But this is false. There is no way you can see me; there is no way I can see you. There is no way I can be sure of this rug beneath my feet. There is no way for me to know that there is a room here. There is no way that I can ascertain that there is a sun, a sky, trees, war, peace, or anything.

Each of us is living in a chamber with several openings that we call "sense organs": eyes, ears, nose, mouth. In this chamber, there is a transparent screen. Behind this transparent screen is a candle flame. This candle flame is self-luminous, as any flame is. It casts illumination on its surroundings. We know that "things" are "there" because we see them illuminated. The visibility of those illuminated objects depends on the illumination cast by the flame. In other words, they are made visible by the flame. Does the visibility or the luminosity of that flame depend on the objects? No! Just so, the world depends upon me—upon my consciousness; I do not depend on the world. The flame is "I."

So let us get back to those habitual self-definitions once more. "I" am not the tall inside the tall woman; "I" am not the skinny inside the skinny man. So, how can someone else's opinion ("Ha, look at the skinny man!") possibly affect me? There is no way that statement or that perception can affect me because I am the unaffected, the absolute, the undying, the unborn.

This is the highest realization in meditation: *In me, time and space stand still. I am condensed eternity. I, pure self, pure light, pure consciousness, am surrounded by a transparent screen.*

This screen is the force field called "the mind." Now the mind has peculiar properties. It can be gross and slow moving, or as fast moving as a master of telepathy who can reach halfway around the world in a moment of time. The mind is in its grossest form when it identifies with the body (*asmita*); but when the mind is in its finest form, it is almost as pure as spirit itself.

Attachment and Aversion *(Raga* and *Dvesha)*

The next two afflictions, attachment and aversion, are intrinsically interrelated. Suffering can arise when we want desperately to attain something—be it something tangible, like a new car that we really can't afford, or something intangible, like the love of someone to whom we are drawn. Even if we do attain the thing we want, our suffering doesn't end. The new car is nice, but not as nice as our neighbor's car; the loved one who agreed to be ours is now attracted to someone else.

And what of the neighbor who has the nicer car? What of the other person to whom our loved one is attracted? They stand between us and our desires, so we hate them! We want nothing to do with them! This aversion is the flip side of our attachment.

You ask if it isn't natural to want certain things and not want other things. How can we stop this kind of thinking? Until pure liberation is reached, it cannot be stopped entirely. But at first, consider it a matter of degree. If you must wish for something, wish to remove the pain and suffering of others. The resulting compassion will ward off hatred.

And what of those who are truly nonvirtuous? What of the wrath you feel toward them? Isn't it justified?

The question to ask here is not whether it is justified, but rather whether your wrath helps you move in the direction of absolute freedom. Your indignation, no matter how righteous, still binds you to its object, doesn't it? The right attitude to cultivate toward the nonvirtuous is not one of condemnation but one of indifference, or neutrality. In turning away from evil, one avoids getting burned.

Fear of Death *(Abhinivesha)*

Fear of death is actually a kind of aversion—one might say the "grand-daddy" of aversions. In fact, dread of death may be understood as synonymous with anxiety itself. It is therefore the root source of all fear.

It is fair to say that every living being experiences fear of death—from the smallest insect to the holiest of holy men and women. To those in my tradition, this is taken as a sign that we have all experienced deaths before and that the remnants of whatever emotional or physical suffering accompanied those deaths have left scars *(samskaras)* upon the psyche. It is also implied in our *sutras,* or scriptures, that, in part, the fear of death results from one's own inner, perhaps unconscious, acknowledgment that one has committed ungenerous acts toward others that may rebound in a kind of karmic boomerang.

But as we work toward wisdom and the obliteration of ignorance *(avidya)* in this lifetime—and as we practice compassion toward others—our fear will lessen. We must remember that the world is finite, while the spirit is eternal; and where there is death, there is also birth.

A Test of Mind

I hope you are still with me after my brief digression into the five *kleshas.* And now I will give you a little reward in the form of a simple self-test.

Remember the question that brought us to that discussion:

> *How do I distinguish what is coming from the unconscious from what is emanating from the inherent absolute freedom and the self-luminous light that I am?*

You will know if you are making progress toward becoming unbound from the *causes of suffering* and receiving wisdom from your authentic Self if you follow this procedure. Let's say you think you have solved a problem. But if the pain in your mind continues long after you have solved the problem, then you have not solved it at all—and you are not free. So long as the shadows keep dancing on the external surfaces of the mind, your internal reality is still the same. You have not solved a problem unless you have solved it in your mind.

You thought everything would be fine if you quit your job and got away from your boss. You quit, but you still think about that job and that boss every day. You think about how you were wronged; you wish you could get revenge; you are afraid the same pattern will develop with your new boss. Are you free? No, because your mind is enslaved.

As you move toward freedom, your mind will achieve a state we call *"chitta-prasadana"*—a state of the mind being in a pleased condition. *Chitta-prasadana* is not the pleasure caused in the mind by something outside the mind, such as "Because I found this new apartment, I am pleased." That kind of pleasure doesn't last very long. Soon you are looking for something else. However, the kind of pleasure that resides with you in Apartment 1 or Apartment 2, or wherever you reside, is the *prasadana* quality. It is like the mind of a very young child. It is the essence of equanimity. . . . It wears a sincere little smile.

In sum, we have identified two areas to cultivate. One is the quality of strength of mind; the other is not being bound by the five *kleshas*. You can test how you are doing. Any problem that you have is a mental problem. If the mind were not disturbed by it, it would not be a problem at all. In trying to solve the problem, what you are actually working on is removing the disturbance of mind. But if the disturbance of mind continues after you have freed yourself from a situation, ask yourself: Have you really freed yourself from that situation?

Eight

A Very Secret Secret

In this book, I have talked a lot about the mind. I have said that the mind is like a strong current of electricity. Yet, although this field of energy vibrates at the highest possible frequency imaginable, the strong-minded person is not a rushed, agitated, impulsive person. Just the opposite: the strong-minded individual possesses the most cherished values of any great religion or system of ethics: gentleness, tolerance, generosity, charity, and love. The strong person is capable of personal creativity and, moreover, is able to nourish and nurture others so that they, too, may create their reality from their truest Selves. This is all because the strong-minded person has access to a reservoir of steadiness and stillness.

In order to help you better understand this last part, allow me to offer another analogy for the mind itself. Imagine your mind is like the sea. On the surface of the sea are many waves. But if you dive underneath the surface and go down a little ways, say a mere fifteen feet, there the sea is so calm and quiet that Jacques Cousteau termed it "the silent world."

So, what is the truth about the sea? Is it choppy and stormy, full of roiling motion that tosses ships about, or is it a vast depth of stillness?

You cannot settle that question with a one-word answer, but you can say that the majority of the sea is silent. The surface alone is full of waves, storms, and tides (notwithstanding the massive ocean currents that, too, flow silently).

This is exactly true of the mind. All the activity of the mind—all intellect, all poetry, all war and peace and treaties, all histories, all constructions from the Pyramids to the Taj Mahal, all cultures of nations, all foods, sex, desires, urges, quarrels, conflicts, and emotions—springs from the *surface* of the mind. But the larger part of the mind's energy lies undisturbed. It is not a shipwrecking, destructive wave of thoughts, feelings, problems, worries, difficulties, and concerns. Although the energy of the surface arises from the depths, the depths themselves—that is, the major part of the mind field, the mind sea, the mind ocean—are always quiet and tranquil.

A Secret Revealed, Yet Still a Secret

After you have read this far, it may not come as a surprise to you that I maintain that the part of the mind I am describing—the still and silent, yet infinitely generative part—can be accessed by meditation. But what I am about to tell you next, I guarantee, will come as a very big surprise. I am about to share a secret with you, although it is a secret of a very uncommon nature: If this secret were announced on the eleven o'clock news tonight in every language, broadcast on every radio and television station and in every newspaper headline around the world, and if everyone heard it and read it, it would still remain a secret. What kind of a secret remains a secret even when told to everyone? A fact about consciousness.

States of consciousness are very, very personal, private secrets. They cannot be conveyed through words, although they may be pointed to with words, and they cannot be exchanged by any two people—no matter how close those people are. You may be close to your spouse, sharing everything, but you cannot ask your spouse, "Please sleep for me tonight. Please dream for me tonight." Your sleep is your own personal state of consciousness; your dreams are your own province. Try cutting out a piece of your dream and inserting it in someone else's sleep. Good luck!

So now I will tell you the secret that will remain a secret until and unless you personally experience and validate it. Ready? The secret is this: From the moment of birth until the moment of death, every person is in meditation, all the time, for twenty-four hours a day. It's a secret like the silent world of the sea described by Jacques Cousteau. If you have never dived, that world is a secret to you. You can read about it, hear about it, see it on TV, but it is still a secret.

So now you have been told that a part of you is always in meditation. What does this mean for you? Does it mean you will be instantly "enlightened"? No. But it means you can stop thinking about meditation as a something induced or learned, or something that involves an "altered state." Think of it, instead, as simply tapping into a natural resource that is already there, abiding. Meditation is a preexisting condition!

Can you look at the ocean from the shore and try to stop the waves? Again, good luck. You can never stop the movement of the ocean's surface. It is a lost cause. But what does the diver do if he dives down to twenty feet or two hundred feet? Does he worry about the surface waves? No, he does not. Is he tossed about by them? No, he is not.

Just so in meditation. The surface waves will go on. Let them. Why are you so bothered by them? The energy that is manifest in each and every one of those waves has risen up from a still and silent world. Simply dive into that preexisting world and all is calm. You need not attempt to make a change in your state of consciousness on the surface of the mind. Just go below it.

Those who are already meditators know that when they are in the state of meditation they often perceive that the mind is functioning on two different levels simultaneously. On the first level of the surface waves, worries and concerns are felt and all kinds of thoughts arise. Nevertheless, there is still a depth, calmness, and silence where the mantra or the object of concentration (for example, the breath) endures. You learn to grab hold of that part—which I remind you is always, always present and available—and plunge into the vast, immeasurable, silent, abiding world of the mind.

And after meditation? You will continue with the duties of your life, but from a deeper part of your being.

The Myth of the Altered State

The secret that I have just told you is one that you still will need to discover for yourself. But once you do, you will understand what a misnomer it is to refer to meditation as an "altered state" of consciousness. In meditation, the consciousness is not altered at all. The stillness beneath the storm is consciousness in its pure, utterly unadulterated form.

The shirt I'm wearing is an altered state of cloth. This cloth is an altered state of thread. The thread is an altered state of cotton. The shirt itself can be altered . . . say, into a rag to wipe with or into a flag to wave. We have a whole series of alterations to the cotton that becomes the thread that becomes the cloth of this shirt. But there has to be cotton in order to have an altered state of cotton.

Another example: You can take gold from a gold mine and produce a nugget. You melt it and you can have an earring, a gold coin, or a necklace. By becoming a necklace, does gold cease to be gold? Of course not. Is there any alteration in the "gold" nature of gold? No. In order for something to be known as a piece of gold jewelry, it first has to be unaltered gold and not something else, such as silver.

As for consciousness, it, too, has alterations. There are three altered states, to be precise: wakefulness, dreaming, and deep sleep. Those are the alterations. They are not pure consciousness itself. The meditative state is the unaltered state that is the essence, the Uncaused

Being—unaffected, unfettered, unexcited—like the still depths of the sea. Pure consciousness is a spiritual force that does not waver.

The mind field in its absolute state is in touch with that unaltered consciousness, with the unaltered state of being. And when this is so, you are beyond any sort of differentiations. For example, at the deepest level, is there a male mind or a female mind? A male spirit or a female spirit? In meditation, no, there is not. The soul, being born as male or being born as female, is not altered into maleness or femaleness. Male and female waves collide only on the surface. Likewise, is there an American spirit, a Chinese spirit, or an Indian spirit? Is there a wealthy spirit or a poor spirit? You see where I am going. At the deepest level, all identifications with such distinctions as gender or nationality or socioeconomic class or any worldly conditions are fakery.

Magnetizing the Mind

I hope I have cleared up some misconceptions about the mind and about consciousness. And now there remains one more matter to clear up. I want to address for a moment the distinction between "activity" and "passivity," because this is related to a number of other important concepts.

We think of action as a kinetic force—that is, as motion. Everybody thinks of Western civilization as an active civilization. Western language reflects this. Meet a Westerner and he will ask you, "How are you *doing?*" Westerners like to go fast, because they equate motion with productivity, success, and prosperity. But to modern physics, the idea of motion as the only form of energy is obsolete. Motion, the kinetic form, is actually the grossest, coarsest form of energy—not the finest.

The finest form of energy is actually the fastest, vibrating at the highest frequency. At this frequency, you reach a paradox where you cannot distinguish the difference between motion and nonmotion. This is the frequency of cosmic rays: ten to the power of twenty-eight cycles per second. If you were moving your hand that fast, you would never notice any motion. Just so, the electrons, protons, and neutrons, the light waves and sound waves in your body, are moving at a rate so fast that you notice no motion on their part.

So now let's get back to the mind. The more the mind calms down, the higher the frequency with which it vibrates. This is a very important point. We experience waves, agitation, and excitations of the mind because we have made it slow down to a coarse level. When we are overcome with negative emotions, we let the mind become agitated—excited in the kinetic sense—and, ironically, this results in a loss of energy.

Think of how you feel when you say, "My mind is racing." You are not "mindful" then, are you? You are not "thoughtful" in the creative sense—even though you are "full of thoughts." You are not prone to notice subtleties and make new connections. And you certainly have no comprehension of things moving at finer, more subtle frequencies.

On the other hand, the mind calmed is the mind energized. There is no wasting of energy.

Think for a moment about a magnet and some surrounding needles. Suppose you lay a magnet down and you sprinkle a box of pins and needles around it. Which is seen to move, the magnet or the needles? The needles! But which is exerting the real force? The magnet, of course. Are the pins and needles more energized than the magnet? They are not. They are reactive. The magnet is generative: It generates the force.

Meditation offers a way to magnetize the mind. That part of you that is always meditating is the most powerful part of you. Don't you want to get to know it better? Why keep it a secret from yourself?

Nine

THE NEGATIVE EMOTIONS:
GETTING THE LEAD OUT

We concluded the last chapter by talking about magnetizing the mind to enhance its power. Yet it must be said that there are some negative emotions that are themselves so powerful they can create a blockage of refined *sattvic* energy. The presence of such an emotion is tantamount to putting a piece of lead—which is nonconducive—on top of a magnet. Such an emotion can cause a warping in the field of the mind.

What is the nature of such an emotion? To start, we have to acknowledge that there are four normal urges shared by all human beings (and all animals). They are:

- the urge to eat
- the urge to sleep
- the urge to fear (which is the same as the urge to violence)
- the urge to reproduce

Also, as my tradition teaches via numerous ancient texts, we have six negative emotions:

- uncontrolled passion
- anger
- greed
- attachment
- frenzy (anxiety)
- malice

The urges and negative emotions combined become destructive when the mind has a strong aversion to or attraction for only one small part of any possible combination of the four urges and six negative emotions. For example, we are greedy about money because of an excess of fear, or we overeat out of an excess of anxiety. That particular overwhelming trait, or "symptom," begins to show itself over and over. It shows itself in thought, in speech patterns, in choice of words and tone of voice, in body language, in the way we sleep and the way we dream. It impacts everything we do to ourselves, as well as all of our actions in relationship to others.

When the expression of one of these traits is repeated often enough, it becomes a habit, even a compulsion. It becomes something we cannot live without (like a constant craving for food, alcohol, shopping, or sexual conquest), or in some instances it becomes something we cannot live *with* (like a certain type of person we cannot stand to be around). Regarding this last point, it should be noted that often the type of person whom we cannot "stomach" is actually someone who demonstrates a trait in ourselves that we don't like and that we therefore attempt to deny and to "swallow."

So, how are we to deal with these destructive habits and compulsions? Nowadays there is an attitude: *That's just the way I am; I have to like myself as I am.* I don't agree with that attitude at all. If I say such a thing to myself, I am stopping myself from growing and from refining my habitual patterns.

It is all right to think, *I have got to like myself as I am,* insofar as other people's opinions and expectations are concerned. You do not want to be in a situation where you are constantly tormenting yourself over other people's ideas about you—especially since you now know that those ideas are frequently colored by their own issues and conditioning. But at the same time, if someone offers a criticism of you, you should be able to listen to it, analyze it, and take away from it what is constructive, thereby bringing a change within yourself. You should not reflexively think, *I'm not going to change; this is just how it is.* Better to ask yourself the question *Why am I the way I am?*

Set yourself a goal to refine yourself constantly and to be a refined person. By "refined," I don't mean someone who can set forks and knives in the right places on a table, or who can tell a Manet from a Monet, or who can name which Beethoven symphony is playing from its first few notes. By "refinement," I mean working toward the basic virtue of being a human being. Something that fulfills you only with regard to the four basic urges and six negative emotions is not refined. However, something that elevates those urges and emotions to become the instruments of the sublime is refined.

There are refined, sublime aims possible behind all of the activities and expressions of our urges. Take, for example, your reasons for reproduction. Do you want to have a child? Yes, you have the urge to do so. When you are married, it is nice to have a child. But do you want to have a child as a decoration—something to show off? A lot of people—though not everyone—have a child for that reason. But the wish to have a child in order that a very pure soul may be born into your family and in order that you may become an instrument for helping him obtain his enlightenment: That is a refined wish.

Take another example: the negative emotion of greed. A lot of people say that it is not good to be greedy, so I am not going to work and earn money—and anyone who makes money is bad. But remember, it is not that act that matters, but it is the act's sublime end. A very ancient instruction in the Vedas, scripture from the fifteenth century BC, says, *Earn with a hundred hands and give with a thousand.* Greed is not overcome by ceasing to earn, because the emotion of greed can be felt just as equally by a beggar, with only a tattered shirt to his name, as by someone with millions in the bank. There is not necessarily any difference between the strength of the possessiveness shown by the two. The way to refine greed is through generosity. If you cannot earn, how can you give? When you earn in order to cultivate the value of giving, then you are using the natural acquisitiveness of the animal urge for the sublime end of giving. You are refining yourself and changing your habitual pattern.

Will you change a habit overnight? Of course not. I talked earlier about the importance of beginning at the edges. Simply by beginning at the periphery of your usual choices—for example, by giving a little more than you have given in the past—you gradually undercut the force of the big habit or the big personality trait that is outstandingly negative and that you previously considered so deeply rooted that it could not be altered. Our compulsions have a support system from which they draw and which they reinforce. However, if you can weaken these associations, the major habit pattern will change, and that will refine you.

There is one word that I do not use often. It is almost as powerful a word in the language of yoga as is "sin" in Christian doctrine. That word is translated as "negligence and slothfulness." We say, do not be lazy! Keep watch over yourself constantly. That is true mindfulness: to witness continually your thoughts, emotions, and actions in order to cultivate purity. Do not neglect or "tune out" those thoughts, emotions, and actions; use them as instruments—the means of attaining a sublime emotion.

It is all right to be flexible. If you cannot do a good deed in one area, do it in another area. If you cannot do it in a major area, do it in a minor area—or in any area where your resistance is not so strong. (If you do not like to give your money, then perhaps you can give your time.) Do that deed selflessly, seeking no reward. Through that deed, whatever it is, a feeling of satisfaction will come to you. You will feel content and fulfilled—that secret, quiet fulfillment like the kind you get when you buy a secret gift and hold it for a month, until it is the receiver's birthday.

I am not talking in clichés: The science of positive psychology has shown that doing good and giving to others is one of the principle causes of personal satisfaction. That is because, as my tradition would say, it is a source of *sattvic*—refined—emotion.

To Hurry Is to Be Greedy

Before leaving the subject of greed, I feel it is important to add one thing of special significance in today's world—especially in the West, but increasingly also in the East. Today so many people are in a hurry to do whatever it is that makes them feel pleasure, I say to them, "Go slowly toward your pleasures." Don't just grab and bite an apple. You miss all of its pleasure. Enjoy it; don't just gobble it. What does the apple look like? What many shades of color are there on its skin? How does its fragrance change as you draw it toward you? How does the surface of its skin feel on your tongue? Now take a bite gently and chew it (as many as thirty-two times!) while keeping your mind not only on its taste but also on all the other sensations it stimulates. Feel the bite of apple go all the way down to your stomach. Now take your second bite. Soon you will see that eating half an apple this way is more satisfying than eating two apples in a hurry.

What applies to one appetite applies to all. Take sex, for example. You don't always have to be in a hurry to give a sexual embrace to show your attraction. Wait, restrain, watch, enjoy. If you made love to a hundred men, a hundred women, in a hundred days, you would learn less about sex than if you took a year, two years, three, of knowing someone—learning about his or her sights and sounds and habits and thoughts and feelings. Imagine if you touched after all of this. Think how much you would understand about making love.

Why all the hurry to "please yourself"? Are you really pleased after you gobble an apple or have a sexual encounter with a near stranger? I don't think you are. Hurry is yet another form of greed. You might never have thought of it this way, but it is so. I see this kind of greed often as an obstacle to meditation. I say, "Lie down and watch your breathing; feel your breath flowing from head to toe." But people are in too much of a hurry to do this. They want to "get on with their life." But there is no life without breath. Now and again, shouldn't we savor the breath?

But what if you do decide to meditate? You schedule it in your busy life and you do it. So, there. You check it off your list. Quite often meditation is not an immediate solution to your negative emotions, or it *is* an immediate solution, but not a permanent one. Meditation will be a permanent solution when your life changes. You cannot really separate meditation from life, so you need to change both. Sometimes I have sipped a drink, and sipped it, and I've refined that drink to the finest possible tickle in my mouth and concentrated absolutely everything on that single taste bud. Then my eyes roll up and I go straight into meditation!

So, to tame your urges, slow down. Learn to recognize your areas of pleasure. Even in the one last apple you eat in your lifetime, there will be plenty of pleasures for all of your senses. To where are you rushing? Relax and enjoy yourself.

Ten

On Money

In the last chapter, I touched on the subject of money. However, because this is such a challenging topic for so many people—and because we are so inclined to tie money into our basic urges and negative emotions—I am often asked to talk about it at greater length.

I think the reason money can be such a trigger point is that nobody knows exactly what money is. You may say that's silly—of course you know what it is! But money is not currency notes; it's not shares of stock. Not really. Instead, it's one of the products of the mind, like everything else in your life. And if you do not understand what the mind is, you cannot understand any of its products.

Means and Ends

Money can be the means to an end. It can be an instrument of generosity, for example, and it can "buy us time" in which to fulfill spiritual goals, such as serving others, and pursuing meditation and prayer without having to worry about how to pay next month's rent. I am a sort of international beggar in that I have had to drum up money from all over the world to support meditation centers, education, and the work of our traveling teachers. Okay, I do it. But I do not do it "for the money." In our lives, we have confused ends and means. We see money as an end in itself. Thrown out of their proper context, the thoughts and feelings you have about money can destroy you and confuse you, leaving you restless and full of stresses and strains. This is all because you don't understand that money and material desires can be inherently useful as servants of virtue and spiritual liberation.

When you lose sight of money's true context as a means to achieving your life's highest purpose—the "true freedom" I discussed earlier—then money itself is your goal. And you can never reach a monetary goal of that sort! One who has nothing wants a hundred dollars; one with a hundred wants a thousand; one with a thousand wants a hundred thousand. He wants a million; she wants a billion; they want to own all the companies in Silicon Valley. And if they own all the companies in Silicon Valley, they want to own all the companies in China and India. They want to own the Earth and the Earth-and-a-half.

You think I am joking, but that's what we are doing. We are trying to own the Earth-and-a-half—or at least the Earth-and-a-quarter. Perhaps you know that every year, we are using up the Earth's resources at a rate of 25 percent more than what the planet is capable of sustaining. We consume so much, and there is no end to our stresses, precisely because we have not set a limit to our desires.

Where is your limit? What is it that you truly need? And for what purpose do you need it? What is the sanest way to meet your needs without doing any harm to yourself or to others—including the Earth herself? Have you ever sat down and figured it out? While you are living this commercially productive life, can you take a little time—fifteen minutes—perhaps tonight, lying in bed? Gift yourself those fifteen minutes, but don't just wander off into a realm of unruly thoughts. Don't examine your true needs when your mind is excited, fearful, and uncertain.

Mind over Money

Remember, everything you do with your life is a product of your mind. Mind is the raw material of everything that you create. Mind is the raw material, not the gold mines but rather the golden mind from which you produce everything. Therefore, before trying to produce this or that, or deciding to enter this venture or that venture, or choosing to make this investment or that investment, calm yourself. Don't do it when your thoughts are confused and when you are emotionally perturbed. Don't do it when your forehead is wrinkled.

Matters of money, like all other matters, must be approached with a calm mind. First learn the art of calming the mind. It's your mind; it's not somebody else's mind. So nobody but you can disturb your mind. I repeat that: No one else can disturb your mind; it's yours alone. So don't say, "So-and-so disturbs me." How could they disturb you? Did they plug a computer into your scalp and download confusion into your head? I say again, it's your mind. You can keep it agitated, stressed, and confused, or you can calm it. It's in your hands, providing you know how to turn its switches on and off.

I digress—"accidentally on purpose," but still—I know you want to hear some more about money. So let me tell you a story about my own hang-ups with money. I am a scholar of the Vedas, and a humble meditation guide. I know nothing about business. I met my guru in 1969 when he was trying to establish his mission in the United States, the Himalayan Institute. All of us disciples were supposed to serve and raise some funds. How does a Vedic scholar raise funds? How was I going to ask anybody for anything? I was baffled, embarrassed—I couldn't do it! So, one day, he said to me, "You have your money hang-ups. What about my mission? Why do you have an inability to ask for money for a selfless purpose?" So after that scolding, what could I do? For a thousand lifetimes, I had been looking for my guru and I found him. Now, just because he gave me my very first task, was I going to walk out on him? Then I might wait for another thousand lifetimes to find him again!

So I had no option. I sat down and thought, *Okay, of all the people in my meditation center in Minneapolis, whom can I ask? Who can afford to give me something?* I made a list of the people in the town where I lived. This person can and this person can—so, okay, I will start tomorrow. No, I'd better start today. The first person on the list was the one I thought was the easiest to talk to. So I went to the phone and was about to pick it up when it started to ring. I picked the phone and it was my guru. He didn't say, "How are you today?" He knew. He said, "Not like that, son. Fix up your mind!"

Well, I don't know who fixed up my mind, but from that moment, clarity came. I had no more doubt or fear. I picked up the phone and dialed the person I'd had in mind and said, "You know my guru is open-ing the Himalayan Institute to teach yoga and meditation. He wants me to raise fifty thousand dollars." (I heard myself say this and thought, *My grandfather never saw fifty thousand dollars in his life!*) Then I added, "Your share is one thousand dollars." That's what I said. The person said, "Oh, okay, no problem."

Really? It worked! He didn't say no.

My path was cleared, once my mind was clear. I had no fears. I had no stresses. I had no doubt. And so, no one said "no" to me.

Then I decided that after raising the first twenty thousand, I would invite all the donors to come for dinner with the guru and I would serve as a waiter. I had it in my head that I might be given a thousand dollars in tips for waiting table and would add it to the sum we already had. But that did not happen. We handed the guru the twenty-thousand-dollar check. After two hours, the phone rang. It was my guru and he said, "Sonny, your wish has been fulfilled. Someone has just given me another thousand dollars."

The moral of the story: When you get past your issues with money and gain clarity, and when you do for others, blessings come.

Settling Your Karmic Debts

MBA courses purport to teach how to make money into more money. But you know what they don't teach? The purpose of making money is to pay off your karma: to pay what you owe to the soul that has become your son or your daughter, to pay what you owe to the soul that has become your father, your mother, your teacher (and, by the way, teachers come in many, many forms). I don't say you must hand stacks of cash to people in your life. I mean to say that you should use money to do what is necessary to help each of them achieve his or her life's purpose. The settling of your personal karmic debts is a most noble purpose of money.

Then, beyond giving to your personally beloved ones, give more. Use your money to fulfill the natural impulse to give. We so often ignore this impulse. We do not share, and that is why we feel so lonely. In all the societies I have come across, in each country and each culture, from Islamic traditions to Western Christianity traditions to Buddhism traditions in China, every spiritual guide teaches that we should give away 10 percent of our income. In English, there is a word for it: "tithing." In Hindi, we call it the *shansh:* same concept, giving away 10 percent. And you know what will happen? If you truly give away your 10 percent, you will get 20 percent back—but don't do it for that reason, and don't do it for the tax deduction either.

When your mind's motive is the pleasure that giving gives you, then your money will grow. Try it and you will see. Even if you do not believe in God, God will give you a blessing.

And while we are on the subject of giving 10 percent, let me suggest some other ways to carry out the spirit of tithing. Did you give 10 percent of your time away today in selfless service? "Selfless" means not only don't you get monetary return, but also that you don't seek acknowledgment. Do this and you will see how your happiness will grow by leaps and bounds.

Now try this: It is relatively easy to sit down to pray every day and do meditation for fifteen minutes or a half hour. But can you make sure 10 percent of your thoughts throughout the day are generous, loving, giving thoughts? Trade a jealous thought for an appreciative thought. That, too, is tithing, and that, too, merits a blessing. Positive thoughts will return to you ten times over or a hundred times over or a thousand times over, depending on the intensity of your thought, depending on the clarity of your thought, and depending on your level of depth and concentration.

So again, I urge you to give and give. If you want to improve your karma, this is the way. Be creative in your giving. Throughout our current lives (and, as we believe in my tradition, throughout our past lives), we have taken on debts. That is to say, people have served us, and people have cared for us. But you would not go back to your mother and say, "Here is the milk I took from you, thanks!" So, how about getting resources to those who need milk and other forms of sustenance now? Your teachers gave you knowledge. Can you pass on knowledge to others? There are many excellent ways to pay your debts.

You are all familiar with ledger books. What you owe is in red (accounts payable); what you are credited is in black (accounts receivable). Everyone wants to be "in the black," yes? Now think of your karma as that ledger book. Remember that fundamentally, the word "karma" means "action"—whether that action is a debt incurred, or something positive that amounts to a credit balancing your account. The wrong actions are debits; the rights actions (generous actions), the right words (sweet, gentle, generous words), and the right thoughts (charitable, appreciative thoughts) are credits. When you act, speak, and think from loving kindness, your credit balance grows. Do you want to know the way to true prosperity? Tilt your karmic ledger toward the black. Tilt it toward love.

Eleven

On Overeating

Just as our urges and emotions can be distorted with regard to money, they are often distorted with regard to food. And just like matters of money, food-related issues can become so preoccupying that they continually distract us from pursuing higher purposes. So let's talk about food.

I am not a medical doctor, and I understand that there may be medical causes for some when it comes to overeating. I am not an expert in these matters; and if you think this is your situation, you should consult your physician. But what I want to talk about here is the psychology of overeating. Why do so many of us have such a craving for food even when we do not require more food? Why are we subject to this craving, this hankering?

It probably is not news to you that issues around eating are often related to issues concerning oral satisfaction, and that this type of satisfaction is connected with the first association we had as infants. We associate the movement of the mouth with a feeling of security inside us. So the fridge becomes a kind of mother figure, a stand-in for the love, sharing, admiration, and appreciation we may be missing in our lives. If you can come to terms with this and acknowledge that *my desire for eating is actually my desire for loving and sharing,* then you can begin to work on that aspect of your psychology.

The first thing you must understand—and we talked about this in the area of money as well—is that human desires are never satisfied. Know before you indulge your appetite: *I am going to indulge this desire, but I am not going to have full satisfaction and fulfillment.* Don't go to the refrigerator or the table with false hope. Go with awareness. I'm not saying don't make that sandwich. I'm saying go ahead and make it, but don't stand there trying to fill the emptiness of your heart and mind by trying to fill the cavity of your stomach.

All right, once you have understood the causes of your internal insecurity and your craving, then what? What if you don't make a second sandwich, but you find you are still lonely? Well, then you must address the loneliness—and, yes, you can do that using food as a tool.

Food Can Express Love for Others

Throughout every culture and civilization in the history of humankind, food has been a vehicle for showing love. This is part of the problem we have with food; ironically, though, it can also be a means to a solution. So when you are feeling lonely and trying to overcome that loneliness, don't do it in a vicarious manner—don't overfeed yourself. Instead, try to make it a practice not to eat alone. And when you have excess food, be sure to give it away.

Maybe you like sweets, as I do. I was born and raised in India, where we have some very rich, delicious sweets you cannot get in too many American cities. When I lived in Minneapolis, I would find these sweets in Chicago or New York. I knew I shouldn't eat too many, but it was a struggle. I asked myself: If I put these in my mouth, will I be satisfied? Well, no. So I took the sweets home to my children—whose metabolism was faster and who could afford to enjoy occasional sweets—and you know what? I was satisfied. I have learned over the years that when I take food and I put it in somebody's mouth, I am satisfied. And I actually lost my own desire for sweets.

In my country, we have an ancient parable. The Lord Progenitor, Father of the Universe, had two groups of children. One consisted of devilish beings (*asuras*) and the other of celestial, angelic beings (*devas*). These groups battled for eons over who would master the three worlds: Earth, Sky, and Heaven. The Lord Progenitor always favored his angelic children, and the other ones grew very jealous and angry. They demanded an explanation from their father, so he said, "All right, let's discuss it over dinner. I invite all of you to come and have dinner at my palace. And, *asuras*, since you always say I don't favor you, today you will be the first to eat."

The *asuras* sat down on both sides of the table. However, before a sumptuous dinner was served, the father's servants took hold of each one of the devilish beings and tied splints from the middle of their palms to above their elbows. The father said, "All right now, go ahead and eat."

But although they tried and tried, they couldn't eat. They couldn't figure out how to maneuver their food into their mouths. They got very angry and complained that they had been tricked.

"Is this what you called us here for?" they cried.

Their father said, "Well, if you don't know how to eat, get up."

After the *asuras* left the table, the father then ordered the angelic ones to sit down. They sat down along both sides of the table and, again, the Lord Progenitor ordered his servants to bind their hands and arms with splints. He said, "All right, begin."

The *devas* ate freely, with each person putting the food in the mouth of the person seated opposite them. They were able to enjoy their food because they also enjoyed love.

So you see the moral of the story. One way to curtail your own overeating is to share your food. Don't eat alone if you can help it. And if you must eat alone, have a thought for those who are hungry. Make it a point that you will gain satisfaction from finding ways to share your excess with them rather than consume it yourself.

Savoring the Savory

None of this is to say that you should not enjoy your food. You should learn to enjoy it more. In fact, one of the main reasons for overeating is that we have not learned to enjoy our food.

There are really only two sources of pleasure: restraint and concentration. Restraint simply means holding back a little. The less frequency for a pleasure, the greater its intensity. When we indulge a pleasure that is available to us over and over again, we become numb to it. (Would it be fun to have Thanksgiving dinner every day?) And when we eat all we want, whenever we want, we lose the ability to tell when we are really hungry.

So don't indulge your appetite to its fullest. Take a vow. Make a quiet resolution to eat three to five mouthfuls less than the amount that would make you feel "full" (three is fine for beginners and you can work up to five). While you continue to eat, you will think, *I am still hungry.* After a few minutes away from the table, however, your desire for more will abate and you will feel perfectly satisfied without being overstuffed.

I have known many people who go on binges of eating and reactive binges of guilt-ridden fasting, but there is no need for extremes. The method I have just explained is a kind of "fasting," because it is based in awareness. So sit for your meal with the awareness of how your body is taking in your food. Soon you will be able to easily identify that "three mouthfuls less" point in your satiety. It is not torture, I promise. In fact, soon you will see that it is just the opposite because as you become conscious of your eating, your concentration will allow you to enjoy your food much more.

With concentration, there is no need to eliminate any one kind of food. Do you like pie? Good! The next time you go out to your favorite diner for pie, go with a friend. Order one piece between the two of you. Enjoy the look of it. Enjoy the fragrance of it. Take a small forkful, put it in your mouth, taste it, and chew it slowly. Concentrate on your taste buds and you will discover textures and flavors in your piece of pie that you have not experienced since you were a child.

There is an art to eating, a technique. Nowadays there is so much focus on what to eat. But not many people focus on *how* to eat. Consequently, our stomachs have become dull, numb, and insensitive. So think about that: *How should I eat?* Your kitchen will become a sacred place, and your body will thrive.

Twelve

ON SPIRITUALITY AND LONGEVITY

Concentration, awareness, restraint, spiritual willpower: So far I have said quite a bit about how these practices can contribute to a higher quality of life. But can they also contribute to a greater quantity of life? In fact, they can. If you wish to prolong your life, you should know that many of the things we have already discussed will help you to do so.

Eat Less to Prolong Life

It is a scientifically tested fact that when you eat less, your metabolism will not have to work so hard. The body will conserve its energy. Eating less in terms of both calories and volume is important, but so is eating less in terms of frequency. I have advised against reactive binging and fasting, but many spiritual paths call for some sort of fasting at regular intervals. If you feel called to fast on such occasions, know that you will be doing a beneficial thing for both your spirit and your body.

Speak Less to Prolong Life

I have mentioned many benefits of silence, and this is yet another. What is speech? Put your hand in front of your mouth and say a few words. Say, "I love you, I love you, I love you" three times. What do you feel on your hands? You feel a jerky breath. That is how speech is generated: by jerking all your internal organs from the navel up. Your lungs, your heart, your voluntary and involuntary nervous systems, your thoughts, and your brain all jerk together simultaneously in order to produce speech. If I were to drive to work every day over a bunch of potholes that caused the carburetor and the wheels and the steering and the accelerator and the brakes to shudder and jerk, do you think my car would hold up well?

Given how much we "waste our breath" in needless speech—especially negative words, gossip, judgments, and criticisms of self and others—the wonder is not that we die, but rather that we are still alive! So make speaking less a goal, and also remember that it is not possible to speak less unless your mind speaks less. If your mind is a chatterbox, your mouth will be a chatterbox as well.

Master Your Sleep—and Replace Some Sleep with Meditation

All across the so-called developed world, there is a widespread phenomenon of sleep deprivation. Nobody is getting enough sleep. But I am not going to tell you to sleep more, but rather to sleep less. Now don't go saying, "Hey, that swami says I should sleep less, so I'm going to take these pills so I can stay up." What I am referring to is taking perhaps two hours of the ideal eight-hour sleep time and using them to practice conscious rest (we call this *yoga nidra*). As for the six hours that remain, two of these can be a two-layer rest where meditation and sleep go on simultaneously—that is, one layer of the mind is sleeping, and the other layer of the mind is meditating.

You may not think this can be done, but that is only because people have very strange misconceptions about the mind. Certain varieties of waterfowl and certain varieties of fish are known to sleep with half their brain at a time—and with one eye open. They rest half their brain because part of them must remain guarding their young. So they have to take conscious rest. If birds and fish can do it, so can you. There are yogic techniques you can study to achieve this—which is not surprising, since, after all, hatha yoga is based on imitation of the animal kingdom. (Think about down dog, pigeon pose, and camel pose.)

We humans are an evolved species, very proud of being at the top of the food chain. So make up your mind to master what other species seem to know instinctively. Make your sleeping time a kind of half-meditation. Here are some simple steps to try: When you lie down at night, do not go into an uncontrolled reverie about your day and your problems. Go into meditation and focus on your breath. If you have a mantra, say it over and over in your mind. From there, lift off into sleep. Then throughout the night, as your sleep shallows out during regular intervals (we all do this as we go through regular sleep cycles), keep your awareness as a meditative awareness by employing these same techniques. Then, in the morning, wake up fully the moment you have the very first dawning of consciousness. Do not let your "mind race" while you are in bed.

Just resolve to keep doing these things and in time your sleep will change for the better. It will happen. Now your sleeping time will not be wasted and you will regulate the depth of your sleep. This, too, can lengthen your life.

Practice Self-Observation at All Times

Witness yourself; observe yourself. What do I mean by self-observation? Do I mean looking in a mirror and asking aloud, "Mirror, mirror, am I looking as beautiful today as I was yesterday? Is that another wrinkle I see?" No, that is not what I mean. (And, as an aside, I would like to point out that the cures to your wrinkles are not in a cream, but rather in your mind.) What I mean by self-observation is taking short periods of time throughout the day (two minutes) to check up on your mind—is it playing any of its many mischievous tricks?—and to check in with your soul—which is the peaceful, nonreactive observer of such tricks and diversions.

In the Vedic tradition, we have a tradition of this kind of contemplation that we referred to as *atma-tattva-avalokanam*—basically, it's an awareness of the principle of the conscious self that underlies you, everyone else, and everything else. (The American transcendentalist Ralph Waldo Emerson referred to something like this when he wrote "The Over-Soul.") From the vantage point of this kind of soul awareness, you will be able to do everything that you ordinarily do—tasting, touching, seeing, hearing, eating, speaking—with greater objectivity and calm. That is because you will be deliberately accessing the layer of immortality that underlies your time-bound "self."

All I ask is two minutes. You have two minutes before you go to bed. You have two minutes when you wake. You have two minutes before breakfast. You have two minutes before you drive off; you have two minutes to sit in your car when you are going for your appointment, for an interview, or to a party. You even have two minutes when you are sitting in a meeting at your office and tempers are rising. What do you do in those two minutes? You switch on your peace mechanism. In your mind, there are war switches and there are peace switches. Actually, they are really the same switches: You lift them up or pull them down. That's all the difference there is between war and peace.

As you gradually develop this habit, you will lessen the number of unhealthy stressors in your life. You will reduce your psychic pains and at the same time reduce your desires or pleasures (which, as we have discussed, are never-ending and therefore themselves a source of pain).

What's more, since *atman* (the soul) is immortal, living in that realm of pure consciousness, while dealing with mortal life, will bring you closer to immortality.

Begin with brief, simple periods of self-observation (what thoughts am I having? how am I reacting?) and gradually your old habits will drop off. Don't worry: You will not be able to reduce *all* your desires and indulgences. You may succeed in reducing them by 10 percent. And rather than being a burden, this will, believe me, be an act of triumph and a source of healthfulness in the truest sense of the word.

Be Where You Are

Many people seem to be under the impression that they can prolong their life by withdrawing from the world. They dream of a day when they can come to a place like my ashram or attend another meditation retreat or perhaps even enter a monastery for a period of time. Maybe they want to—literally—withdraw to a cave in the mountains. But if you have such longings, you have to ask yourself: *What will I do when I get to my place of retreat? Will I only sit there in body as I wander the world in my mind?*

My guru used to say, "When people are at home and busy with their businesses, they keep saying, 'I'll go to the ashram. I'll go to the ashram,' and the moment they get into the ashram, they start thinking about the business they left behind."

Why can't you be in one place at a time? Make up your mind. When you are here, be here. When you are there, be there. That is a far better way not only to elongate your days, but also to make each day a thing of value.

Be exactly where you are. When you catch your mind wishing you were anywhere other than where you are, that is the perfect time to flip your switch to the "peace" position—your deepest inner awareness—and examine your desire from a place of calm objectivity. What is the difference, really, between "here" and "there"? All places are one place. The difference is in your mind. As the wise yogi Vasistha said, "There is nowhere where you are not."

A Word About Illness

Despite your best efforts to remain healthy, there remains, of course, a chance that you may develop an illness. What can that signify? And what are you to do?

According to the *Charaka Samhita,* the oldest classical text in India's Ayurvedic medicine, all disease arises from "a failure in wisdom." That is a unique way to look at illness, isn't it? God doesn't send diseases to strike you down because God is a vengeful God.

If you develop an illness, you should treat the illness. And, of course, you should do what you can to minimize the impact of that illness on your life. But one thing there is not much point in doing is asking, *Why me? Why did God do this to me?* Look at the situation from this new perspective and consider that your actions, your karma, your accumulated desires, played a role in what has manifested as illness.

Now, wait, don't go thinking that having an illness makes you a "bad" person. That is not what I am saying at all. I am saying that every action that takes place, everything that happens to you—illness included—can be seen as a lesson.

Disease is often an indication for a change in your life. As you contend with your illness, see what it has to teach you. And even when it causes you discomfort (dis-ease) remember that you are paying off a debt, after which you will feel clear, relieved.

I have had my share of physical illnesses, but I know that pain is only a signal and that illness is a great source of knowledge. These things help me to understand my body. They help me understand how my mind controls my body, and I use that knowledge for helping others.

Illness and pain can cause hardships, yes, but they can also give you time for reflection, prayer, and meditation. If you are lying in bed, call on your positive emotions and go as deeply as you can into meditation. I have had some medical procedures—like angiograms and angioplasties—where doctors have had to put all kinds of tubes in me so they can look around and tinker. Two or three hours go by and everyone wants to know: "Are you okay? Are you dead?" No, I am in ecstasy! Three hours with no phones, no appointments, no e-mail!

While the doctor was doing his work, I was doing mine. I was practicing *yoga nidra*—the type of conscious rest I mentioned earlier. And in doing this work, I actually prolonged my life.

I wish I could teach this practice to all doctors to teach to their patients. Patients who use "sick time" for prayer and meditation will come out of the hospital and heal more quickly. Some of them will cut their hospital stays in half, with the right emotions generating the right flow of *prana* (life energy).

If you develop an illness, make the most of it. It's an opportunity to get God's attention, as you give more attention to God.

Thirteen

What Are You Waiting For?

N ow we have talked about living a longer life, but we have not really addressed the most important question linked to that topic. Like most everyone, you wish to live a long life. Why?

Yes, why? What is the purpose of that life you wish to prolong? Imagine you are sitting in a car and you start driving. Where are you going? You don't know? All you know is that you want a long trip. Doesn't that seem odd?

Why do you want to stick around on the Earth? To complain? To get even? To accrue money and things when, as you know, "you can't take it with you"? Maybe you just want to go on living because you have a fear of death. But fear of death is not a purpose, is it? That would mean you are simply living because you are scared of the alternative.

So, first of all, let us stop living in fear. Think about it. Really. Deeply. Why is it that you want to live long?

Some people might say they want to live long so they can make as many people happy as possible. That is a good purpose. The longer they live speaking kind words and doing selfless service, the more people they will make happy.

You can make this goal even wider. How about this: The longer I live, the more time I have to realize the perfection of the Divine. To die without having seen a glimpse of God, to leave this body without having realized the Truth—it's a shame. It's a great loss.

A Wave in the Universe

But let me backtrack a little bit. In order for you to arrive at such a purpose, first you must accept a certain underlying premise. Put simply: There is a reason that you are here in this world. You are a wave in the vast, huge karma of the universe. You are responsible for your experience and you are capable of altering it. Remember the story I told earlier: You can create your own Heaven, even when you find yourself in Hell.

By altering your feelings, your "reality," you alter the experience of those around you, making it possible for them to do likewise. That is how your tiny being affects the entire universe.

All of us are on a path to perfection. No matter how many detours we put in our own way, this is still the path we are on. Nevertheless, a moment will come when this body of yours will be terminated. Forget about all those stories you have heard where you must account to someone else at that juncture. At that moment, you account to yourself.

At *this* moment, you may say, "I've still got forty years." And you avoid thinking of what might happen at the end of those forty years. You don't want to hear about death and the unpleasant things that may precede it (the old belong in senior citizen homes; the dying belong in hospitals). You don't want to acknowledge the journey on which your mortal body has embarked since the moment of birth.

Come face-to-face with that now. All the saints, all the religions, all the prophets, have instructed, "Whatever you will do with your mind at the moment of death—do that right now." And then, when the next moment arrives, do the same. Do your personal accounting: Did I come any closer to perfection in this lifetime? Did I contribute to happiness, joy, and love? This particular feeling that I have *right at this very moment:* Is it conducive to that perfection? (If not, then that feeling is a ticking bomb—get rid of it! Throw it away!)

Yes, I know that feelings cannot be changed easily, because behind those feelings is the momentum of our *samskaras,* our accumulations of past conditioning and patterns. However, we must always remember that alongside our seemingly indelible psychic scars, there is within us an ability to exercise will. And that willpower can apply brakes to this momentum. You can say, "No, I am behind the wheel of this car and I am changing direction."

Let your spiritual willpower win out over habit.

The Power of Intangible Goals

In your life, you probably have many tangible goals. You need to provide for your family, put your children through college, keep your physical body in shape, and so on. Of course you need to attend to such things, but your intangible goal may be missing.

"What good is an intangible?" you may ask. Well, what good is a smile? That is an intangible. What good is love? That, too, is an intangible. We might take intangibles for granted, until they are missing, and then we recognize how imperative they are.

But developing intangible goals in life is really only possible when you have a philosophy of life. You have to do this for yourself. The U.S. government is not going to establish a Department of National Philosophy. It's not complicated. Suppose you choose a personal philosophy based on three Sanskrit words: *satyam, shivam, sundaram* (truth, goodness, beauty). Then you gradually begin to assimilate the philosophy into practice by applying it to specific decisions. Then you will attract the kind of people who are looking for the kind of actions you exemplify.

Do you think this is oversimplified? Try it out and you'll see. A cliché is a cliché when we don't want to practice it. When we want to practice it, it becomes a philosophy.

Enlightenment in this Lifetime

Every teacher, everybody who teaches in the name of God or the soul—anyone who tries to elevate the human heart to be pure, to be unselfish, to be Divine—says that the moment to decide to commit one's life to the intangible goal of benevolence, love, and purity is not seven years from now, or seven months from now, or seven days from now. The moment is now, this minute. There is no time to lose. To paraphrase a Sanskrit verse: *While the body is still firm, while the senses are still strong, while old age is yet distant, while you still have a life span in front of you to devote to something self-constructive and creative, take this moment—now—to raise your sights and say, "I will make this self a glorious, Divine Self."*

Don't wait until your house is on fire to dig a well. Don't put off making your decision until the day after tomorrow. There is always a reason to postpone your aspiration. (You might have heard the famous saying "Lord, make me good, but not yet.") And keep in mind: Next year's reasons for procrastination will be just as valid (or invalid) as today's.

Now I'm not saying that you should go and join a monastery or renounce the world and become a wandering swami. The form your aspiration takes will vary from time to time, according to your growth and development. Nevertheless, you must always allow in your mind the possibility that it's actually feasible to become Christlike or Buddha-like.

It's possible to become enlightened in this lifetime. It *could* happen.

In this very life, you could have a glimpse of the highest wisdom. That is because there resides in you a natural tendency toward goodness, an inclination toward enlightenment, because of the very nature of your being—the Divine spark within you. *The very spark of life within you is the link with Divine life.* The link cannot be broken. Once you have this idea settled in your mind, then you can begin to aspire to enlightenment.

And what will it be like, this enlightenment? Well, I will tell you what it will not be like: It will not be a state of longing and craving. For however many moments you are in the enlightened state, you will want for nothing. You will look at all the gold, silver, and jewels of the world and see that they are meaningless. You will understand that you can possess nothing, that nothing is "yours." This will not bother you—just the opposite. The only thing that will matter is the central core of your being. The knowledge of being inextricably linked to the Divine will cause you to rejoice completely.

Can you think of anything more worthwhile? Can you think of a work of art or architecture, a beautiful piece of clothing, the greatest glory ever attained by a conqueror or an emperor or a politician, that is more lasting and more fulfilling than this knowledge? I cannot think of it.

But first there has to be an aspiration, an aspiration to glimpse this knowledge, this deep understanding. And let it be a quiet aspiration—for goodness that declares itself is not goodness, but ego. Forgo the ego. Accept that you are not the "doer" of your life, but a channel through which the source of all things is flowing.

Will you still have problems in your life? Undoubtedly. And there has to be a determination to accept whatever "problems" may arise as opportunities to pay off your karmic debts so that your path can be cleared. That is what problems are for. Pay off your karma and it will be like paying off your mortgage after thirty years. It will be cause for celebration.

What will not help is if you use your problems as excuses to postpone your aspirations. You want to straighten out your life? I know of nothing short of the pursuit of Divine linkage that straightens life out completely. I know of nothing short of total aspiration for infinite Truth that removes all wrinkles, erases all stains, and eliminates all strains and conflicts from one's mind and one's relationships. I know of nothing else that will make you free.

A Final Word

There is a story in India, and in many other traditions as well, of a wandering saint. The saint arrives in a village and everybody comes to see him and invites him to stay with them. Most everyone is happy, feeling inspired by his presence and finding some peace of mind as a result of his public talks. But there is one man who remains very sad, so the wandering saint asks him, "What is wrong?"

The man says, "Master, I am sad for my brother. He is the village drunkard. He doesn't want to come anywhere near a saint, a temple, or a spiritual teaching. He won't come to see you, even though he is deep down very talented and lovely, and listening to you might keep him from wasting his life. He only goes to the wine shop."

The wandering saint leaves the village for a time. When he comes back, he brings a signboard. On the outside of the cottage where he stays, he hangs the sign, which says: THE NEW VILLAGE WINE SHOP.

So that village drunkard walks by and notices the signboard. "Oh, when did they open this one? I have got to try it." He walks in and his eyes meet the eyes of the saint, and something clicks. The drunkard embarks on a path toward enlightenment.

So these wandering saints and swamis are master tricksters, me included.

I have talked about many worldly matters in these pages—from how to communicate with others to how to manage your emotions to how to deal with food and money and illness. But underneath it all, I really have one goal: to get you, the reader, to find the value in silence and meditation—so that you can bring forth your spiritual willpower, cultivate positive thoughts, and seek wisdom that leads to ultimate Truth.

The moment your blocks are removed through mental relaxation, through stilling the mind, all kinds of good things will begin to happen—things you won't believe. You may call these things "flukes" or "accidents" or "random chance." Or you may call them "miracles." You can call them whatever you like. This old trickster will not be bothered.

And now, allow me to share one final thing with you. If someday you begin to get a very distant glimpse of God, you will find out that everything that is written in books—everything that is taught by the priests, the mullahs, the swamis, and the monks—and everything you have heard about God is lacking. If you have a distant glimpse of God, you will find out that God is just not like that at all.

"Oh, Swami, what is God like then?"

You want the answer?

To that question, silence alone is the answer—not just silence of words, but the peaceful, shining silence of your mind.

Acknowledgements

M y sincere thanks to the following individuals: Arlene Matthews (book editor), Judythe Sieck, (book cover design), Dr. Mehrad Nazari, Shi Hong, Bhola Shanker Dabral, Stephanie Finnegan (copyeditor), Erica Wilder (contribution to book cover) and Michele Hebert.

Made in the USA
San Bernardino, CA
22 August 2019